HOW TO GO WILD

DOMINIC UTTON
ILLUSTRATED BY DAVID SEMPLE

SCHOLASTIC

For Albert and Eithne — my own wild things

Text copyright © Dominic Utton, 2012
Illustration copyright © David Semple, 2012
All rights reserved

ISBN 978 1407 13034 7

Printed and bound by CPI Group (UK) Ltd, Croydon, CR0 4YY

2 4 6 8 10 9 7 5 3 1

The right of Dominic Utton and David Semple to be identified as the author and illustrator of this work respectively has been asserted by them in accordance with the Copyright, Designs and Patents Act, 1988.

Papers used by Scholastic Children's Books are made from woods grown in sustainable forests.

CONTENTS

INTRODUCTION

If you live in a town or city, it's easy to forget about the wild. Our solid brick and concrete buildings, our roads, trains and subways, the instant warmth, light and clean running water we can get from the flick of a switch or the turn of a tap ... sometimes it can really seem like we have conquered nature completely.

But don't believe everything you see around you! Even in the biggest cities, you don't have to go very far to get away from human civilization. Just look at a satellite pictures of the Earth from space: in even the smallest countries, our towns and cities don't actually take up as much space as you might think. There's still an awful lot of wild out there!

And did you know that there are even still parts of the planet that remain totally unexplored by modern man? It's amazing – but it's true. There are areas of the Amazon jungle in South America as well as the wild lands of Papua New Guinea that remain untouched by everything we take for granted.

Scientists and explorers are still discovering people living in these places, people still living the way our ancestors did thousands of years ago.

Now, you're unlikely to go exploring the Amazon just yet (unless you're really, really lucky!) but that doesn't mean you can't have your own wild adventures right outside your window. Wherever you live, you're never more than an hour or two from open countryside, deep, dark forests, fast-flowing rivers, rolling hills and steep valleys – all waiting for you to explore them and all places where you need to know the skills in this book in order to get by.

And even if you can't get out into the open wild just yet, there are still plenty of techniques to learn in your back garden or local park, whether it's pitching your own tent or learning the best fishing techniques.

So what are you waiting for? Get stuck in! Enjoy this book – and then use what you've learnt to truly go wild!

Safety and responsibility

The wild is a beautiful, exciting, wonderful place, crammed with incredible adventures just waiting to happen ... but it can also be a dangerous place. Never embark on any trip without first letting an adult know exactly where you're going and getting their permission. Let them know how long you plan to be and ideally take them along with you.

This book also contains tips and techniques on subjects such as care for your penknife, and how to make a bow and arrow. All of these come with legal warnings — be sure to read and understand these properly.

You should also be extremely careful around fire — practise all the techniques you learn here with adults before you ever attempt them by yourself. And remember that fires can get out of hand very quickly. **ALWAYS** have a water supply handy and be quick to put out the flames at the first sign that it's getting out of control.

Remember: the wild can be a great adventure, but with that adventure comes responsibility. The true adventurer not only loves the wild, he respects it.

That means you must try to leave it just as you found it.

• Never harm animals – it's not only against the law, but it's cruel!

• Try not to damage trees and other plants. You want to leave the wild as you found it – ready for others to enjoy as much as you do.

• Always pick up and take your litter with you. Plastic bags, sweet wrappers and bits of fishing tackle can all cause harm to animals.

• Always be aware that you are just a visitor to the wild. Keep your eyes and ears open for danger – from sudden changes in the weather to wild beasts!

And lastly – and most importantly – have fun!

TRUE TALE: Alexander Selkirk

Robinson Crusoe is one of the most famous survival stories ever written. But did you know it was based on the true adventures of a Scottish sailor?

In 1704 a navigator named Alexander Selkirk was abandoned on the island of Juan Fernandez, an uninhabited speck in the Pacific Ocean, after arguing with the captain of his ship. All he had with him was a loaded pistol, a knife, a hatchet, navigation instruments, rum, food for a few days and his Bible. There was no escape – the closest inhabited island was 600 miles north. But Selkirk was determined to survive. He explored the island, and found water, fruit, shelter, and wild goats to hunt. Once, he chased a goat off a cliff. The fall knocked him unconscious for three days, and he'd have died if he hadn't landed on top of the goat.

After four years and four months, a British ship spotted the smoke from Selkirk's fire and Selkirk was rescued. He became a celebrity in his hometown of Largo, where the writer Daniel Defoe heard his story. After Defoe published his account of Selkirk's adventure – retitled *Robinson Crusoe* – both men became famous worldwide. Sadly, Selkirk never really adjusted back to life away from adventure. In 1720 he joined the ship HMS *Weymouth* as first mate, and died on board a year later.

BEFORE YOU GO WILD

Getting ready for your adventures is not only important, it's also great fun! There is loads of stuff to do before you go wild — from the obvious things to getting your kit together and checking your equipment, to learning some vital tips and techniques that should help make you a better and smarter adventurer once you're away from home.

In this section you're not only going to learn about all the practical things that need to be done just before you set out, but you'll also learn some skills you can practise in the times when you can't get away. If you use your time between adventures cleverly, then you'll have so much more fun once you are out in the wild again!

Packing for your adventure

Every expedition – no matter how big or small – starts with the planning. When you're out in the wild, you have to rely on what you've got with you. There's no popping back indoors to pick up a forgotten essential and no shops nearby to stock up on supplies. If it's not in your pack, it's not in your pack!

Even if you're planning on simply camping out overnight in your back garden, or hiking a short way from home, it's a good idea to prepare as if you're going deep into the wilderness. You never know when the good habits learned will come in useful for real!

The important thing to remember is that you can only take what you can comfortably carry. Be ruthless – because any non-essential item will be taking up the space of something far more useful.

Try to think of ways of making your pack as light as possible. You can take food out of its packaging, for example – but remember to cut out and keep any instructions you might need.

Backpack essentials

Every adventure's different and each one needs its own special equipment in your pack. But even for but the shortest hikes, there are some items that are essential. Keep the following packing list handy every time you go wild: tick them all off as you pack, and make the tick into a cross when you unpack again at the end of your expedition.

Water – at least two litre bottles, freshly filled

Water is the most important thing your body needs to survive – always take as much as you can! And remember, in extreme hot or cold conditions, you will need to drink more.

Water purifying tablets

For when you cannot find or collect fresh drinkable water in the wild. These can be found in most camping shops.

Matches – in a waterproof container

Plus a lighter. Remember to make sure you know how to use them safely, and always let an adult know you have them.

Watch

Not only for telling the time, but as you'll discover, can also be used as a compass in the wild.

Mobile phone – fully charged

For emergency use! Make sure you have useful numbers programmed in – and that responsible adults have your number too. If you have space and can afford one, you may want to investigate solar-powered phone chargers on the internet, too.

First-aid kit (see p. 156)

Make sure it's up-to-date and anything you've used has been replaced. This is essential kit – never leave home without it!

Sunscreen

Sunburn can be very painful and dangerous, so make sure you've got a good high-factor sunscreen with you. And, of course, if you're going to be in hot conditions, remember to pack enough to keep putting on more sunscreen throughout the day.

Whistle

For attracting attention in an emergency. Can be worn on a string around your neck – this not only saves space, but means it's always handy.

Torch – and spare batteries

For seeing in the dark!

Pocket knife (see p. 21)

Knives can be very useful – but must be treated very carefully. And again, make sure an adult knows you're carrying one.

Magnifying glass

Believe it or not, this can be used for starting a fire!

Candle

Just in case your torch batteries run out.

Compass

If you know how to use a compass properly (see p. 15) then you'll never be truly lost in the wild.

Maps

Make sure you've studied them thoroughly before you leave. It's a good idea to keep them in a clear, sealed plastic bag (large sandwich bags or freezer bags are ideal) – this will keep them dry and clean.

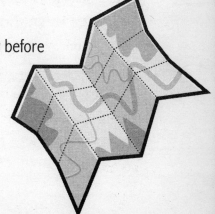

Binoculars

Again, these can be worn around your neck. Great for spotting potential trouble before it sees you … but also brilliant for getting a closer look at the wildlife around you!

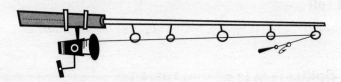

Fishing line, hooks and floats

As you'll see on p. 103, you don't need to take your whole rod and tackle in order to catch fish! A good length of line, a selection of hooks stuck into blu-tack and a couple of floats all safely sealed in a tin are ideal.

Food rations – including Kendal Mint Cake and chocolate

Nothing tastes as good as campfire cooking! There are plenty of techniques and recipes in the 'Campfire cookery' chapter. And the Kendal Mint Cake and chocolate are great for boosting energy, especially when the terrain is tough or in extremely cold conditions.

BEANS

BEANS

Tinfoil

Fold up two good lengths (a square about as long as your arm from elbow to wrist should be enough) and put them with your food. Very useful for cooking!

Strong, lightweight rope – as much as you can carry

Rope takes up a lot of space, but is incredibly useful for making all sorts of essential things in the wild.

Toilet roll

Make sure it's environmentally-friendly and biodegradable.

Extra clothes – at least one spare set

Keep them dry in a plastic bag and change clothes whenever you get soaked. Wet clothes are not only heavier, but they can quickly give you a chill and lead to more serious illnesses.

Hat

Essential in all weather conditions! When it's hot it will keep the sun off your head, when it's cold it will help keep you warm, and when it's raining it will make sure you stay a bit drier!

Cooking utensils: two pans, mug, cutlery

Camping shops sell kits that all fold into each other – they are ingenious and brilliant for saving space in your pack.

Sleeping bag

Get the best you can afford – especially if you plan to be sleeping in extreme conditions!

Tent

Again, invest in the best you can. Your tent is all that stands between you and the wild when you're asleep — the last thing you want is for it to collapse in the middle of the night!

Journal

This will record your movements, journey, sightings and any other observations. For more on keeping your journal, see p. 30.

SURVIVAL TIP!

If rope is too expensive or bulky to carry, a washing line can be used instead. It's not ideal — but it's better than nothing!

WARNING!

A good penknife is essential kit for every adventurer — used in everything from cooking to building shelters. But it should also be handled with extreme care. Make sure your parents or guardian is fully aware that you have it with you — and that they are happy you know how to use it and care for it properly. By law, all carried knives must also be able to fold away and be no longer than seven and a half centimeters long. For more on knives, see p. 21.

Making an adventurer's staff

A good stout staff is essential for any true adventurer. From the first cavemen to Ray Mears and Bear Grylls, the best explorers have used one of these simple but priceless tools in the wild. Whether it's as a walking stick, a tool for testing things from the depth of water to quicksand, a means of knocking down apples from high branches or even a weapon for fighting off angry wild animals, a staff has as many uses as you can think of for it.

And of course, they're great for walking – especially in hilly or mountainous areas, where a staff can actually keep you stable along treacherous paths.

How to make your own staff

You want your staff to be strong enough to survive anything you use it for – but not so heavy that it's a burden to drag around with you.

1. Find a good solid branch of wood – yew is ideal – about your own height.

2. Try the branch for weight first: don't be afraid to keep rejecting potential staffs until you find one that feels right.

3. Once you've got one that feels perfect, trim off any branches with your penknife and whittle down any rough knots.

4. If you can get hold of some sandpaper, give it all a good sand down so it's nice and smooth. This will help protect your hands against splinters and blisters.

5. Finally, give it a name. It's going to be your faithful companion on all your adventures: so your trusty staff deserves a name of its own!

SURVIVAL TIP!
You might like to record your adventures on your staff by carving symbols into it – one for each time it has come in useful. After a few trips into the wild it could end up covered in ancient-looking runes like a wizard's staff...

Your knife

For years, a penknife has been an essential part of every adventurer's kit. However, recently, a lot of crime involving knives — sadly, some of it by kids — has meant that knives are under the spotlight as never before.

Because of that, it is **VITAL** that you always obey the following when it comes to knives.

- Only use knives under the supervision of an adult.
- In the UK it's against the law to sell a knife to anyone under the age of 18.
- Any knife you own must have a blade of less than seven and a half centimetres and be able to fold away.
- Make sure that you have had plenty of practise with your knife before you go on any adventure.
- Take care of the blade. Keep it clean and folded away.
- **ALWAYS** make sure you know where your knife is. Pack it away whenever it's not being used.
- Only ever carry a knife with the permission of a responsible adult. And only ever carry it when you are in the wild. You must **NEVER** carry a knife around day-to-day.
- Last, but most importantly, be careful! Knives are very useful in the wild — but they are very dangerous too!

Clouds and weather

Every trip into the wild is dominated by the weather. Knowing what the weather is going to be like can be the difference between having a great adventure and spending the whole time thoroughly miserable.

It's not simply a case of warm weather good, cold weather bad, or dry good, wet bad … if you can predict what the weather is going to do then you can plan properly – and be prepared to make the most of whatever happens.

In the scorching desert, for example, being able to spot the signs of a rare rain shower can mean the difference between surviving and disaster. And in ancient times, sailors who could predict the strength and direction of the wind would see their ships reach the safety of land first.

Of course, nobody can get it right all of the time — some of the world's greatest adventurers have fallen foul of unpredictable weather changes. But a little bit of knowledge — and a few simple tricks — should at least give you a bit of an edge...

Cloud spotting

The easiest way of predicting the weather is to look up and see what the clouds are doing. Their height, size and even colour can give you essential clues...

Thin and whispy, white, high in the sky

These mean fine, dry, sunny skies for some time to come.

Large, billowy, white clouds

Can be a sign that rain will arrive soon — but not immediately.

Blanket of grey, dull, low in the sky

Believe it or not, this doesn't necessarily mean rain. Grey clouds in the morning often clear by lunch to reveal blue skies. But afternoon clouds like this are a more sure sign of wet weather to come.

Thick, dark, very low

Expect a long, gloomy downpour. If it's not raining already, it will be very soon!

Large, very tall, dark underneath and white on top

Take cover! There's going to be a storm! The more impressive these cloud towers look, the fiercer the storm will be...

Simple forecasting

Even in the wildest, most remote corners of the world, you can still have access to some of the most reliable weather forecasting known to man. And, for the really smart adventurer, you don't even have to be able to see the sky to know what's going to happen!

• Look for wild flowers. All plants love rain – but flowers are especially sensitive to a good soaking! When nature senses a shower, many flowers will close their petals in anticipation to protect the pollen – tulips are an especially good indicator.

• Watch the birds. Can you see any? If the answer's no – especially if they had been around earlier – it almost certainly means rain's on the way. This is because the worms and insects that birds eat will all have taken shelter.

• So if you can't see birds ... listen for insects! Are the mosquitoes out? Are the bees buzzing? Lots of insects mean dry weather – and no insects mean rain on the way.

• Check the tops of trees. The branches here are lighter and more sensitive to the wind. They will sway before anyone on the ground feels a storm blowing up.

Extreme weather

Occasionally, mother nature throws some seriously nasty weather our way – and when she does, the effects can be devastating. It's a good idea to know what to do when the conditions turn bad…

Floods

"Flash" floods can strike quickly and devastate an area within minutes. They are also very dangerous: not only could you drown, but the raging waters can carry heavy objects which could cause serious injury. Look out for the following signs of a flash flood…

• Floods follow rain – but often strike further downstream than the original downpour. Try to be aware of the weather at all times: if you hear thunder upstream, be especially cautious.

• Keep an eye on any streams or rivers nearby. If a clear stream suddenly becomes muddy, a flood is on its way.

• Watch for stream and river levels. A sudden rise is bad news!

What to do in a flash flood

1. Move to higher ground. The higher the better, and as far away from water as possible – just 10 cm of moving flood water can knock you off your feet.

2. Once you've found a safe place stay put and if necessary, signal for help (see p. 26).

Tornadoes

Tornadoes are incredibly powerful funnels of air that can cause massive destruction. They hit very quickly and without much warning, but you can look out for some signs that a tornado is coming.

- The sky turns a deep greenish-black colour, often very quickly.
- It suddenly starts to hail.
- Look at the clouds — are they moving very fast, twisting into a cone shape? Tornadoes are called "twisters" because of this.
- Listen: tornadoes make a roaring noise that will get louder as it gets closer.
- Are branches dropping from the sky? The tornado is close!

What to do when a tornado strikes:

1. Run. As fast as you can. A tornado is very fast, so it's best to go sideways, out of its path, rather than trying to outpace it.

2. Find a ditch, or a hollow and lie face down, with your arms over your head.

3. **NEVER** shelter under a tree — they can be sucked into the tornado!

Thunderstorms

Although the chances of being struck by lightning in the wild are slim, it does happen! Every year in America alone, around 50 people are killed and 300 injured by lightning. Although nowhere outside is truly safe in a thunderstorm, you can take precautions to keep safe.

• Keep an eye on the weather. Look out for clouds with dark underbellies (see p. 24).

• Watch the insects and birds – they usually disappear before a storm hits.

• Learn how to tell how far away a storm is (see below).

How to measure the distance of a thunderstorm:

If you can hear thunder and see lightning, you can measure how far away the storm is from you. This is because light (i.e. the lightning) travels faster than sound (the thunder).

1. When you see the lightning flash, start counting slowly: the best trick is to count "elephants" – "one elephant, two elephants, three elephants," etc.

2. Keep counting until you hear the thunder. The number of elephants you've counted to is roughly the number of miles away the storm is!

3. Next time you see lightning, do it again. Has the storm moved closer or further away?

What to do if you're caught in a thunderstorm

1. Don't panic! Staying calm is the best way of staying safe.

2. Get away from isolated spots as soon as possible. Lightning will usually strike the tallest point, so if you're on a high plain or on top of a hill, get to a more sheltered spot.

3. **NEVER** shelter under a tall tree. Not only will it attract lightning, but you could be hit by falling branches.

4. Find a low spot away from the wind, such as a cave, or between rocks.

5. Stay away from power lines and electric fences. Lightning conducts electricity and will be attracted to these.

6. Water will also conduct electricity so keep away from streams, rivers or lakes.

7. Crouch down on the balls of your feet with your hands over your ears.

How to keep an adventure journal

One of the most important pieces of kit you'll use on your adventures will also be something you create yourself. An adventure journal is a record of all of your expeditions — as well as a handy how-to guide for future trips. In it you should write everything that happens, as well as any new skills and techniques you use or problems you solve. Your journal should, of course, include plenty of drawings and photos from your trips. Your journal should go with you everywhere and you should always be ready to add or refer to it — just think, in years to come you could be turning it into a book for future adventurers eager to pick up on what you've learned on your expeditions!

JOURNAL TIPS!

- Use a spiral-bound notebook, as the pages are easier to turn and refer back to.
- Use a strong piece of string to tie a pencil to one of the spirals – that way you'll always be ready to write in it.
- Keep it somewhere handy in your pack so you can get to it easily.
- Keep your journal in a clear plastic bag when you're not writing, to protect it from wet and dirt.
- You can even make a hole in the bag, loop some string through it and keep it round your neck, so it's always handy.
- Remember to make maps as you go. For more on making maps see p. 40.
- Make time at the end of every day to update your journal with any new adventures you got up to or skills you learned.
- Record where you are, how far you've travelled, where and when you stopped to eat, what wildlife you saw, and so on.
- Take a note of what time the sun rose or set.
- Make a sketch of any unusual features in the landscape around your campsite ... just in case you later get lost.
- Always remember to date every entry!

TRUE TALE: Marco Polo

Marco Polo is one of the greatest adventurers the world has ever known. He also wrote one of the first and best adventure journals!

Marco Polo was born in Venice in 1254 and when he was 17 he set off on a great journey, all the way to China. By the time he arrived at the Chinese court of Emperor Kublai Khan, he'd been travelling for three and a half years and had covered 5,600 miles. The Emperor was impressed, and for the next 17 years he sent Marco on special missions throughout China, Burma and India — some of the places he visited wouldn't be seen by another European for over 600 years.

Marco eventually left China to escort a Mongol princess to Persia. But the journey was disastrous — they were attacked by pirates, hit by disease and faced terrible storms. In the end, of the 600 who set off, only 18 people survived, including Marco and the princess.

Marco made it back to Venice in 1295, 24 years after he had set out — but his adventures weren't over yet! Three years later, he took part in a battle against the rival city of Genoa. He was captured and put in prison, and one of his fellow prisoners urged him to write down the stories of his travels. The result was *The Travels of Marco Polo* — a bestseller across Europe. It was so fantastical most people didn't even realise it was true!

NAVIGATING THE WILD

The very first thing every adventurer needs to know is how to find their way around in the wild. You could be the best at pitching a tent, an expert at lighting a fire, or a master of foraging for food … but if you can't navigate then it's all for nothing.

There are three key factors to surviving and thriving in the great outdoors. You need to be able to find your way:

- Around the wild
- To shelter
- To food and water

In this section you'll find out about the skills you need to navigate the wild successfully and confidently — and then in following chapters you'll see how they tie in with setting up a campsite, and foraging for your own food and water.

How to use a compass

More than any other piece of kit, your compass is the key to finding your way about in the wild. As long as you know how to use your compass properly, you can even navigate in areas without your map!

SURVIVAL TIP!

Compasses come in all shapes and forms, from tiny toy versions like you might get in a Christmas cracker, to super-expensive models used by the military. While anything that points north will do in an emergency, the best kind to get is a standard orienteering compass. Not only do they do everything you'll need, they won't blow your adventuring budget!

Using an orienteering compass is easy.

• The first thing to remember is that the needle will always point north. Forget the N / E / S / W marks around the edge for now — it's the needle you want to concentrate on.

• To take a reading, simply stand still, hold the compass flat and let the needle spin freely. When it stops spinning, it will be pointing towards magnetic north.

• Keeping the compass level, turn the dial around the needle until the N for north mark is directly above the needle. Now the east, west and south marks are in the right places too!

- Use the direction of travel line at the tip of the compass to work out exactly what direction you're going in.

- Line up the north needle with the north direction on your map (most maps point north anyway).

- This means that as long as you can take a compass reading, you'll always be able to make sure you're going in the right direction.

SURVIVAL TIP!

Compasses work by magnetism – so make sure there's nothing magnetic nearby that will mess up your reading.

True north vs magnetic north

The North Pole (or "true north" as it's sometimes called) is actually in a slightly different place than magnetic north – the place to which all compasses point. This is because the Earth isn't exactly round, but slightly flattened at the poles. Unless you're happening to be trekking through deepest Arctic, however, the difference is too small to worry about!

Finding north without a compass

Even in the most remote wilderness, the experienced adventurer should never find himself lost. In an emergency – let's say you've somehow lost your map and compass – finding your way back to your camp, or back to civilization, can be simple.

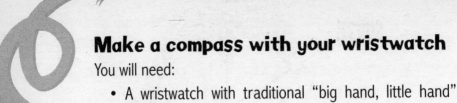

Make a compass with your wristwatch

You will need:

- A wristwatch with traditional "big hand, little hand" clock face
- OR a digital watch and piece of paper, a pen or pencil
- A sunny day!

This is an old soldier's trick, dating back to the earliest watches: all you need is to know the time, and to be able to see the sun. (It doesn't even matter if you have a digital watch — simply draw a clock face telling the correct time on a piece of paper.)

1. If you're in the Northern Hemisphere, point the hour hand of your watch (or your picture of a clock) towards the sun.

2. Find the middle point between the hour hand and 12 o'clock.

3. That middle point is due south — which means north is the opposite direction!

In the Southern Hemisphere you point 12 o'clock at the sun — and north is the middle point between 12 o'clock and the hour hand.

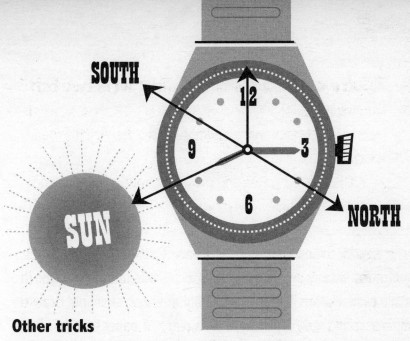

Other tricks

If you find yourself in a real emergency — without even a watch — the wilderness still holds some clues you can use to navigate. All of these should be reversed when you're in the Southern Hemisphere.

• Look out for mountains: the snow on top will always be thicker on the north side. This is because northern slopes get less sun than southern slopes.

• Flowers always lean towards the strongest light — and because the sun is always due south when it's at its strongest at midday, that means that most flowers face south.

• The north sides of hills tend to be damper than the south — because as they get less sun, the dew takes longer to burn off.

• And always remember the golden rule: the sun rises in the east and sets in the west — and at midday will be due south.

Map reading

Learning to read a map can take time – but practise enough and you'll be able to look at a map and see a whole picture of the countryside in your mind.

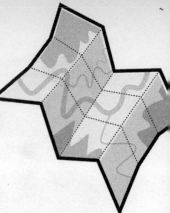

Scale

All maps are drawn to scale. Although it can seem a bit confusing at first, understanding that scale makes reading maps much simpler. Put simply, all scale means is what 1 cm on the map means on the actual ground. So, for example, if the scale is 1:10,000 – that means that every cm on the map is the same as 10,000 cm on the ground – or 100 m. Likewise, 1:25,000 means every cm is worth 250 m.

Contours

These are lines on your map (usually kind of wiggly circles). They join points on the map that are the same height – and help us work out where hills and mountains are. When the contour lines are far apart, that means the ground is sloping up slowly – when they are close together, that shows a steep slope.

Key

All maps come with a key, showing what all the little symbols mean. It's worth memorising a few of the more important ones before you set off so that you don't have to keep referring back to it.

Compass

Maps generally point north – but if they don't, they will come with a compass symbol in one corner indicating where north is. The first thing you should do when reading any map is to line up your compass with the map, so that you know you're facing the right way to read it!

How to make a map

You will need:
- A compass
- Squared paper
- A pen or pencil

Being able to make your own map is brilliantly useful: if you accurately record where you've been and what's around, you can make sure you'll never get lost. You'll also be able to add useful information that less detailed or less up-to-date maps don't contain.

To make your own map, all you have to do is learn to convert measurements in the "real" world to measurements on the paper you're drawing your map on. And of course, use your compass!

1. The easiest way to make an accurate map is to use squared paper. In one of the top corners, draw the four points of the compass, with north pointing upwards.

2. Now using your compass, turn until you're facing north yourself. Now your map and compass are aligned!

3. Next, you have to decide your scale. For the simplest maps, make each square worth one pace — or the distance you cover in one normal stride.

4. You're ready to start making your map! It's a good idea to start with a symbol for your tent in the middle of your map.

5. Then, starting from your tent, count the number of strides to your fire (for example). Now you know exactly where to place the symbol for your fire! Let's say you measured eight paces east to the fire. Simply count eight squares to the right (or east) of your tent symbol and draw a fire symbol.

6. Keep measuring in this way to note down everything you think is useful. And once you leave camp, you can keep measuring out distances and directions as you go!

SURVIVAL TIP!
Using a one square = one pace scale is perfect for a small map, such as one of your camp, but you might run out of space on your paper quite quickly for bigger ones. For larger maps, experiment with one square for 10 paces, or for maps of even bigger distances, 20 paces.

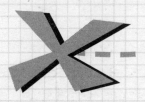

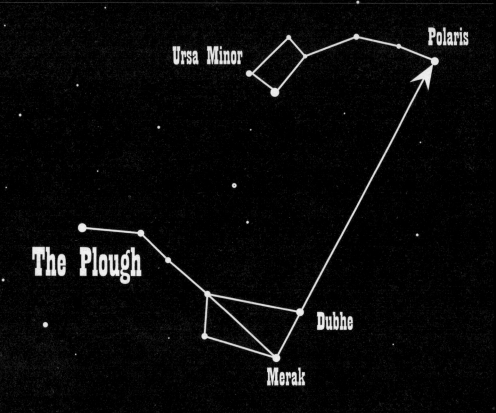

Navigating by the stars

Just because the sun has set, it doesn't mean that you're automatically lost until dawn! In fact, a clear night can make for an amazing permanent compass in the sky — not only is it totally accurate, but you only have to look upwards to read it.

This is because stars don't stay put in the same position all night, but move across the sky like the sun and the moon. All except for one star! And that star just so happens to lie directly above the North Pole. If this star is directly above your head, then, congratulations, you've reached the North Pole!

All you have to do to find north is simply work out where this star (called the Pole Star) is. And, luckily, it's not only one of the brightest in the sky, it's also the easiest to find.

SURVIVAL TIP!
You can also work out compass directions when you're in the Southern Hemisphere (see p. 44).

Southern Cross Constellation

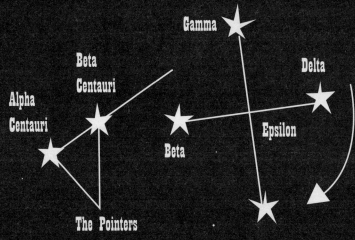

Finding the pole star

The Pole Star can be easily found by first spotting The Plough — it looks like an enormous saucepan. Just draw an imaginary line from the two stars that make up the outer edge of the pan, and the next bright star you see is the Pole Star. Whenever you face this, you're facing north.

SURVIVAL TIP!

In the Southern Hemisphere, the constellations are all different. But to find due south, look for the Southern Cross.

Draw a line down from the middle of the cross itself, and another from the two bright stars on its left — where they meet is due south.

TRUE TALE: Leif Ericson

A thousand years ago, the Vikings, or "Norsemen" (meaning North-men) were Europe's greatest adventurers, sailors and navigators. Perhaps the greatest Norse explorer of them all was Leif Ericson. In 1001, he is thought to have been the first European to discover North America: some 500 years before Christopher Colombus.

Leif sailed from Norway with 35 men, in a boat that seems tiny by today's standards, and crossed the Atlantic Ocean, travelling over 600 miles further than anyone had gone before.

The Vikings still believed that the world was flat, and that if you sailed too far west, you'd reach the edge and drop off. Leif wasn't so sure: he'd learned to read the stars and realized he could navigate by using the Pole Star. He also used a "lodestone" – a magnetized lump of rock that could act as a compass. The way Leif saw it, if he ran into anything that looked like the edge of the world, he'd simply turn his ship around and sail back to Norway.

After months at sea, he navigated his way safely to a land of rich pastures, rivers filled with salmon and lush, dark forests. He called it "Vinland", meaning land of wine – we now know it to be Newfoundland, in Canada. In America, October 9 every year is still celebrated as "Leif Ericson Day" in his honour.

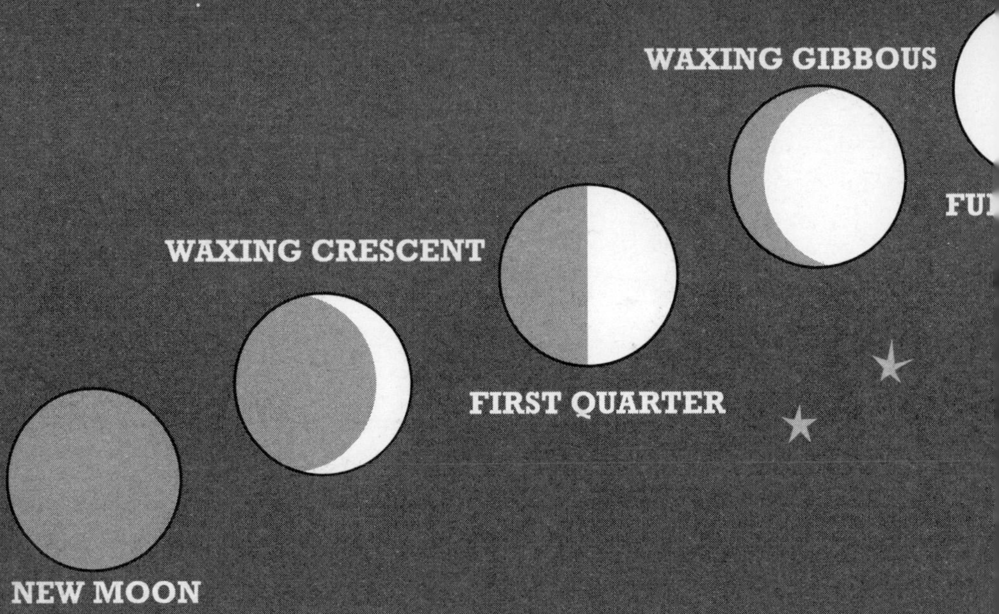

WAXING GIBBOUS

WAXING CRESCENT

FIRST QUARTER

FU[

NEW MOON

Phases of the moon

We've all seen the difference between a full moon and a crescent moon, but did you know you can actually keep a calendar simply by recognizing what shape the moon is?

The different shapes of the moon are called the "phases" of the moon. The moon's shape changes because as it moves around the Earth, the Earth leaves a shadow across its face. Over the course of about a month, this shadow gradually decreases, going from totally covering it (a new moon – when the moon is invisible) to not covering at all (a full moon). The shadow then grows again, until the moon vanishes as a new moon once more.

WANING GIBBOUS

OON

LAST QUARTER

WANING CRESCENT

NEW MOON

Using this knowledge, you can measure time by what the moon is doing. As it takes about a month to go from new moon to new moon again, we can work out that means it's roughly a week between each phase – new moon to half full, to full moon to half full again, to new moon. Very useful on long treks!

SURVIVAL TIP!
The "hunter's moon" is the name given to the full moon nearest the autumn equinox of September 21. It's called this because at this time the moon rises almost as soon as the sun sets – meaning hunters could continue to track their prey long into the night...

Make a sundial clock

You will need:

- A large flat piece of wood (around 40 cm across)
- A pen or pencil
- A penknife
- A stick
- A clear, starry night

If you find yourself in the wild without a clock, you can use an old American Indian trick to tell the time, just by using the sun.

1. First of all, find a smooth, flat piece of wood about 40 cm across and draw a circle on it large enough to fill almost the whole of the surface.

2. Then divide the circle into 24 equal parts — like slicing a pizza. These are your clock hours.

3. Place it on a solid, level surface like a tree stump and fix it as securely as you can — the clock won't work properly if it moves!

4. Wait till it's night and find the Pole Star in the sky (see p. 43). Line up the top line with due north — this will be your 12 o'clock marker.

5. Carefully make a notch in the middle of the dial with your knife.

6. Now wedge in a stick at an angle so that when you look along the stick it points directly at the Pole Star.

7. In the morning, the sunlight will cast a shadow on your stick — wherever that shadow points is (roughly) the correct time!

TRUE TALE: Harriet Chalmers-Adams

One of America's most important explorers is also one of its least well-remembered. But 90 years ago, Harriet Chalmers-Adams was famous as the most fearless female adventurer of her time. She was also a brilliant tracker and trailer.

When she was just 14, Harriet and her father trekked for a whole year through California all the way down to Mexico. It gave her a love of living outdoors, and she was to dedicate the rest of her life to adventure.

She married Frank Adams, an engineer, and in 1904 they set off on a dangerous trip through South America. They travelled on horse, and relied on the skills Harriet had learned as a child to survive. Throughout her adventures, Harriet kept detailed journals – recording all the places she visited, everything she saw, and all the different tribes and cultures she encountered. They were later published as books.

In the 1920s, the National Geographic Society did not allow women as members, so in 1925 Harriet set up her own adventurers' club: The Society of Women Geographers. Shortly before her death in 1937, the *New York Times* newspaper wrote: "Harriet Chalmers-Adams is America's greatest woman explorer".

Tracking and trailing

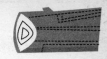

Learning how to follow a trail is an essential skill for the expert adventurer. A tracker is someone who knows how to spot a trail — and can recognize what kind of animal made the trail, how recently, and whether it might lead to food. Anything that makes a trail that a tracker follows is called a "quarry".

The key to becoming a top tracker is to use your senses.

Your eyes

Use your eyes to spot vital signs that every hunter needs to recognize — from the largest footprint to the tiniest blade of bent grass.

Your ears

Carefully listen out for your quarry. Useful sounds could be anything from the noises the animal makes (that lion roaring — how loud is it? Is it close or far away?) to the rustle of leaves and the snapping of branches that might mean something is very close.

Your nose

Your nose isn't only for smelling your prey, but also for identifying the clues it leaves behind ... some of which can be very smelly!

Your fingers

Use your sense of touch can give clues as to how fresh or old a trail is. Let's say you come across an abandoned campfire. Are the embers still warm? If so, it probably means the people you are following are still close by...

The art of stalking – techniques and tips

Becoming an expert tracker can take years of practice – but there are a few tricks that every apprentice hunter can use...

• Use your senses! They're your first and best guide.

• Keep a guide to animal prints handy. In time you'll recognize them at a glance, but at first it helps to have something to refer to.

• It's easiest to track in wet or snowy conditions – because footprints show up better. In dry weather, early morning dew can help the keen tracker.

• Look out for signs of activity other than prints. Animal droppings, broken vegetation, chewed plants and scratched tree trunks are all signs that your quarry may have passed this way.

- Some animals can even be identified by their droppings! And although you shouldn't touch them, some expert hunters can tell how close an animal is by how warm its droppings are!

- Stay quiet and low to the ground – you don't want to scare your target off.

- Keep an eye out for regular trails. Many animals use the same routes through their terrain, just as we make roads – they may be smaller and harder to find, but they're there!

- Look at the distance between prints. If they're close together, whatever you're following is walking – if they're further apart, it's running.

- Concentrate on the ground about five metres ahead of you – you'll move more quickly and spot more sudden turns this way.

SURVIVAL TIP!
Although prints spaced further apart generally means an animal is running faster, remember that the bigger an animal, the bigger its stride! Be careful that you don't end up mistaking something slow and massive for something small and running!

Animal tracks

Recognizing an animal's footprints is the first step to following their trail – and, of course, will let you know if it's the kind of animal you really want to get anywhere near at all!

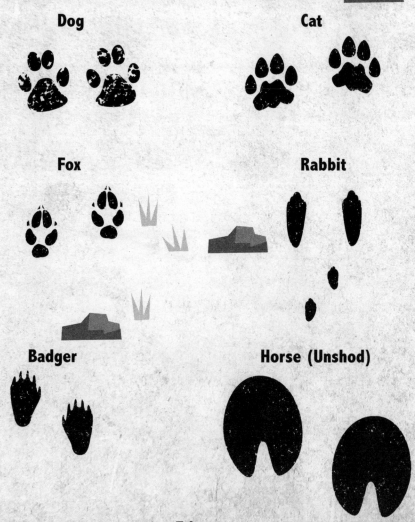

Dog

Cat

Fox

Rabbit

Badger

Horse (Unshod)

Deer

Bear

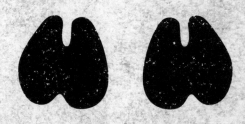

Lion

Camel

Tiger

Elephant

Field signals

Communicating in the wild isn't just a case of pressing a button on your mobile phone. For centuries experienced woodsmen and explorers have managed to signal and leave messages to each other – when out of earshot, or even when miles apart.

Leaving a secret trail – and learning how to follow one – can be very useful if you become separated from your fellow adventurers. Even if you're in an area where mobile phones can't get a signal, you can still leave important clues to your movements. Here are a few of the most common signals – but you can have fun making your own and practising them in the park with your friends.

Sticks bent to the left
Turn left

Sticks bent to the right
Turn right

Crossed sticks
Not this way

Sticks in a triangle
Proceed carefully – danger ahead

How to make smoke signals

American Indians used smoke signals to send messages over distances too far to hear — or even see — each other. Because smoke rises so high and can be seen so far away, a smoke signal can be like painting a message right across the sky!

Making complex smoke signals takes years of practise, but the basic idea is simple.

1. Make a fire. To increase its smokiness, put green wood, moss and leaves on and don't let the blaze become too fierce.

2. Wet a blanket.

3. When you're ready to send your message, carefully throw the blanket on the fire and wait until the smoke stops.

4. Then — being very careful again — quickly pull the blanket off and then put it back on. This will send one puff of smoke into the sky — which your fellow adventurers or tribesmen will understand to mean whatever code you're using (see below for some ideas for a code).

5. You can do this a few times to send two-, three- or even four-puff messages. Any more than four puffs might dry out the blanket too much … and you don't want to end up burning the thing you're sending messages with!

Sample smoke signal code

- One puff — I'm OK!
- Two puffs — Stay where you are!
- Three puffs — Come to me!
- Four puffs — Emergency! Send help!

Semaphore

Semaphore was a messaging system developed by ships' crews in the 19th century. It uses a system of two flags and can be brilliant for getting important messages across distances when you can still see each other ... but can't hear.

If you haven't got flags you can make your own — simply tie the arms of a spare shirt to a stick or fallen branch. Or in a really tight spot, a couple of good leafy branches can work too.

Here are each of the flag positions showing how to spell out each letter of the alphabet.

ERROR   READY!   A   B

Signalling for help from the air

In an emergency — if you're lost in the wilderness, or one of your party is injured and needs assistance — you may need to attract attention or signal for help from the air. The best way is to light and keep a fire going — the smoke from a fire can be seen for miles.

SURVIVAL TIP!

To make your fire as smoky as possible, add leaves to it as well as wood – and once it's going strongly, damp leaves and moss work especially well. Be sure you don't smother it completely though!

You can also use rocks, sticks and whatever else might be lying around to make the universal sign for help – SOS (commonly thought to stand for Save Our Souls). Anyone spotting this sign will know you need help.

Remember – you must never use an SOS signal unless you really are in an emergency! And be sure to destroy your SOS sign once you have been rescued!

PART 3: LIVING IN THE WILD

With the right skills anyone can live in the wild. Once you've mastered the art of getting around, you need to know how to make the most of the natural world to get the most out of it. The trick is not to think of it as a battle for survival against the wild — but learning how to work with it.

Everything you need to live in the wild can be found all around you. Even in the most untamed wilderness, the skilled adventurer can use the land around him to get by. The key is knowing how and where to pitch camp, how to get a fire going, and how to find fresh water.

Your campsite

Think of your campsite as the little spot of the wild you have claimed as your own. It should be clean, safe, and provide you with everything you need while you're staying there. A good site can be home for as long as you need it to be — a bad site will make even the simplest things like eating and sleeping seem so much harder...

Selecting a good spot

The most important thing about a campsite is that it gives you shelter from the weather. Here are a few dos and don'ts to look out for when scouting around for a good spot.

DO: Pick a spot close to running water for washing and cooking. A small stream is ideal, a big, fast-flowing river can be too dangerous.

DON'T: Pitch your camp too close to the water! It is a good idea to try to stay on higher ground, just in case of flash floods.

DO: Take a moment to step back and try to imagine your campsite in the worst possible conditions. Try to imagine any dangers before they happen.

DON'T: Camp next to a lake or pond. Still or stagnant water attracts midges and won't be as clean as running water.

DO: Look for signs of animal activity. Scratched trees, droppings and shredded vegetation can all be signs that the spot is used by bears, big cats or other dangerous animals. See animal tracks on p 54 for more on this.

DON'T: Trample, cut or break bushes and branches unless you really have to. It's important you leave your site as close to how you found it as possible.

DO: Look for a spot close to plenty of fallen and dead wood – great fuel for your fire.

DON'T: Camp in a hollow. In a downpour the water will collect in the hollow and you could wake up to a flood.

DO: Try to select a flat spot to pitch your tent. Your tent will not only be more stable, but you're less likely to roll out in the middle of the night!

DON'T: Camp at the top of a hill. Hilltops are more exposed to bad weather – and in a strong wind your tent may get blown away!

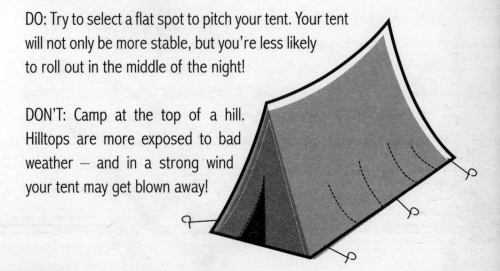

Clearing your site

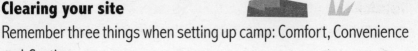

Remember three things when setting up camp: Comfort, Convenience and Caution.

Comfort

Before you pitch your tent, take a good look around. Which direction should your tent face? Would you like to catch the last of the evening sun? Then have it with the opening to the west. If you prefer to wake to the dawn streaming through your tent flap, then face east.

Clear out any stones from the area you intend pitching your tent on. You could spread a "blanket" of comfortable pine needles under your tent area, too.

Convenience

Keep your site big enough to comfortably contain everything you need – an area for sleeping, a spot for cooking by the fire, another area for washing, a spot further away for the toilet. Think of it like organizing a house – with a kitchen area, a sleeping area, a living room, a bathroom, and so on. But don't make it too big – you don't want to have to get up and walk too far unnecessarily!

Caution

You will have looked out for natural dangers when you chose your spot, but be careful not to make any more trouble for yourself. Make sure there's a decent space between your fire and your tent, for example — fires can spread quickly and you don't want sparks jumping on to your tent. (For more on fire safety see p. 82). You also want to think about making sure you don't attract wild animals or insects — see below for some good tips on camp hygiene.

Camp hygiene

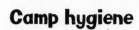

Good hygiene is more than simply keeping the place tidy. If your campsite isn't clean and organized it's more likely you'll get sick, attract unwelcome wildlife, and lose vital equipment in the mess.

Keep clean!

Create a special place in your site for washing pots, pans and cutlery — and a separate place for washing yourself. This will stop you transferring your dirt on to clean cutlery or pots. Running water is **ALWAYS** better than still water — and remember to use plenty of soap. Unfragranced is best — as a strong soapy smell might attract curious bears and other animals. And if you can get the environmentally friendly stuff too, so much the better!

Toilet area

Keep your toilet area well away from anywhere you prepare or eat food. Try to make it downwind of your camp, too.

How to make a camp toilet

1. Dig a hole well away and downwind of your camp. Make it at least 60 cm deep and a little less wide than your toilet bowl at home.

2. Keep the dirt piled up in a little mound next to your hole.

3. This hole is your toilet — for number 2s only! (If you need to wee, you can simply go behind a bush!)

4. Every time you go, simply bury your business (and toilet paper) by tipping in a little of the dirt from the pile next to your toilet.

5. If you are in an area with pine trees, a layer of pine needles will help disguise the smell too.

6. Once you have filled your toilet to within about 20 cm from the top, tip in the rest of the soil and make a new one.

Stay tidy

Clear up plates and wash up as soon as possible after eating – and pack everything away when you're not using it. Rubbish and food scraps left lying around can attract ants and insects ... or bigger animals! This also makes moving on much easier.

Leave as you find

It's important that you leave your campsite looking as close to how it did when you arrived as possible. Take any rubbish with you, carefully put out your fire and clear up any wood or stones that you have collected.

SURVIVAL TIP!

Store all food in sealed containers in plastic bags and hang them from a tree branch slightly outside and downwind of your camp. That way the smell is much less likely to bring hungry bears or other wild animals into your camp.

Making a bivouac

A bivouac is a temporary shelter made out of things found in the wild. If you ever find yourself without a tent and need to get under cover, you can make yourself a pretty good bivouac just using branches, leaves and moss.

1. First, find a long, straight stick about one and a half times your own height. Lean it against a fork in a tree with the other end on the ground. This is the roof of your shelter.

2. Collect more sticks of all lengths and lean them against your main roof stick so you're making a kind of tunnel of triangles.

3. Weave in as many smaller branches between your upright sticks as you can. You want your frame to be as sturdy, strong and weatherproof as possible.

4. Finish off any gaps by stuffing them with moss and dead leaves – and then lay some heavier branches on top.

Making a snow hole

In very snowy conditions you may not be able to pitch your usual tent. In these situations you've got to make shelter – and fast. The easiest method is to build a snow hole. It should get you through the night until you can set about being rescued in the morning!

1. It's easier to tunnel into a slope of snow than to dig straight down. Find a large, stable-looking slope for your snow hole.

2. Start by using a shovel to dig a tunnel about one metre long into the slope.

3. When you've finished your tunnel, set about widening the inside. Simply keep scraping away at the snow at the end of the tunnel until you've got an area large enough for you and your equipment.

4. Try to keep the entrance as narrow as possible – the less cold air that can get in, the better!

5. Be careful to keep the roof as thick as you can! After all that hard work, the last thing you want is for the whole thing to collapse.

6. Use some of the snow you've scraped away to make a bench to sit on: it will be warmer than sitting on the floor.

7. Place a couple of big sticks above the entrance to your snow hole as a marker for any rescue teams that might be looking for you.

8. Finally, place your pack in front of the entrance — though be sure to leave some ventilation!

TRUE TALE: Jo Gjende

Two-hundred years ago, Norway was a true wilderness — a land where reindeers, wolves and, according to legend, giants and trolls ruled. But in the 19th century, one man made the untamed land his own.

Jo Gjende was born in 1794 and both his parents died when he was a child. Raised by his aunt on a farm, he worked hard on the land every day and grew up to be exceptionally strong. In his twenties, he left the farm and headed off into the mountains, looking for adventure. For the rest of his life he lived alone, roaming across the Norwegian wilderness.

Jo loved the solitude of surviving in the wild. In the summer he'd make bivouacs from fallen branches and sleep looking at the stars, and in the winter he'd dig himself snowholes. He always made sure that his campsites contained everything he needed — and nothing he didn't need — and that he could move on whenever he wanted.

When he was about 40, however, he settled down and built himself a log cabin at the mouth of a river. By this time, his reputation had grown: people came from miles around to see him and learn about living in the wild. After his death in 1884 his home-made log cabin was preserved as a tourist attraction. You can still see it today, near the town of Gjendesheim.

Making rope ladders

The beauty of a rope ladder is that it allows you to climb up areas that you wouldn't otherwise be able to — and once you're up there, you can draw up the ladder so nobody can follow you!

SURVIVAL TIP!
Make absolutely sure that whatever you're climbing up can take your weight!

There are many techniques for making rope ladders — but the simplest to make, easiest to stow away and quickest to both put up and get down is the knotted rope method.

1. To make a knotted rope ladder, all you'll need is a good length of strong rope and a fairly hefty stick.

2. Tie regular knots in the rope — try to make each one about the length of a standard school ruler apart. These are the knots you'll be using to climb up and down, so it's worth taking your time to get this right.

3. Tie one end of the rope to your stick and use this as a weight to lob it over whatever it is you plan on climbing.

4. Grab the stick and untie it again — and then tie that end of the rope into a loop (see p. 87 for tying knots). Thread the other end of the rope through the loop.

5. Pull the non-loop end tight. You should see the loop "travel" up the rope until it reaches the top — and then hold tight. You're ready to climb!

The trick to climbing a knotted rope ladder is to take it very slowly until you get used to it! Keeping your knees bent, rest both feet on the bottom knot, raise your hands to a knot above your head and pull your whole body up until you can raise both feet to the next knot together. Simply repeat all the way to the top, remembering to keep both feet on the same knot as each other and your legs bent all the way up!

SURVIVAL TIP!
Never slide quickly down a rope — you'll burn the palms of your hands. Not only very painful, but will also make climbing up again almost impossible!

Treehouses

Treehouses are great fun — but it is important to think of safety. It can be a long way down! Building the kind of treehouse you can sleep in is something that's best left to the experts, but it can still be possible to use your rope ladders to help you use trees as a place to hide, a lookout spot, or simply a refuge to get up and get away from it all for a while.

SURVIVAL TIP!

There are tribes in Papua New Guinea who live their whole lives in treehouses! The Korowai build whole villages at the top of tall trees in the jungle. They even have wars against rival treehouse-dwelling tribes.

Fires

A well-built fire can be your best friend in the wilderness. It gives you warmth, light, safety from wild animals, as well as a way of cooking your dinner and boiling your drinking water. And of course a good fire gives you an excellent place to sit and swap your best wild adventure stories in the evening! In very cold conditions knowing how to light a fire can mean the difference between life and death.

SURVIVAL TIP!
Always keep your matches dry – preferably in a metal tin – and use them as sparingly as possible. However, even if they do get wet or run out, an expert at living in the wild can still get a blaze going.

The best sites for fires

• Position your fire in the centre of your campsite – think of it as your kitchen and living room all in one.

• Clear an area of about 2 m around where you want your fire. Try to clear the ground as possible and keep this area free of sticks, twigs, pine cones or anything else that could catch light. Watch out for overhanging branches that could also catch light!

• To contain your fire, dig a trench or build an earth bank around it, to stop the fire from spreading where you don't want it to.

• On wet or snowy ground, build your fire on a platform of green logs. These will help stop the damp ruining your dry kindling.

How to build a fire

Start small and slowly build your fire up in three stages: tinder, kindling and main fuel.

1. Tinder. This is what gets the fire started. Your tinder needs to be a very fine, very dry material that burns easily. Scrunched-up paper, tree bark, dry brown grass and dried moss all make great tinder. Place it in what will be 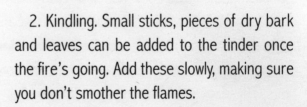 the centre of your fire and once it catches alight, you're ready to move on to the next stage.

2. Kindling. Small sticks, pieces of dry bark and leaves can be added to the tinder once the fire's going. Add these slowly, making sure you don't smother the flames.

3. Main fuel. As the fire gets stronger, keep adding fuel — making the sticks gradually bigger as the flames grow larger. Build them like a pyramid, rather than just chucking the lot on top — if you have the biggest logs on the outside of the pyramid, they will fall on to the flames as the fire burns.

Lighting a fire without matches

Of course you will have packed matches as part of your essential kit — but what do you do if you lose your matches? Or they get wet? Don't worry. Although using matches is by far the easiest way of getting a blaze going, it is still possible to start your fire without them — using the tricks and techniques of old adventurers.

With a magnifying glass

You can use the heat from the sun to get a fire going. It takes a bit of patience but after a bit of practice you should be able to get pretty good at it!

1. Simply aim the glass so the light from the sun is concentrated on to a small spot on your tinder.

2. The sun's rays will make this spot get hotter and before long you should see a thin wisp of smoke!

3. That's when you carefully add more tinder, gently blowing to get the fire going.

4. If you don't have a magnifying glass, a mirror or even a pair of glasses will also work.

With flint

Flint is a type of stone that causes sparks when struck against another piece. Some camping shops should supply them — or you could even ask at the nearest garden centre whether they have some.

Flint can also be found in the wild: look for broken, slate-like pieces of jaggedy rock that looks whitish on the outside and shiny grey-black on the inside. The easiest way to work out if it is flint is simply to strike two pieces together — if there are sparks, you're in business!

1. Scrape two pieces of flint together very fast to make the sparks. You could try scraping it against some metals too. Anything that makes a spark!

2. Patiently keep making the sparks, aiming them at your dry tinder.

3. It can take a while, but if you keep at it you should get enough of a flame on your tinder to add more kindling and get a proper fire going.

Fire safety

As we've already found out, fire is probably your most important friend in the wild. It gives you warmth, safety, comfort and a way of cooking your sausages ... but it can also be your most dangerous enemy. It only takes a few moments for a fire to get out of control – and the consequences can be disastrous.

Always be **VERY** careful when dealing with fire. Here are some safety guidelines that even the most experienced adventurers follow.

- Always get permission from the landowner before you start a fire – and make sure a responsible adult knows what you're doing.
- Keep an eye out for any warnings – for example, many national parks and forests won't allow fires after a long period of dry weather.
- Make sure the area around your campfire is clear of anything that might catch and spread the blaze. This includes overhanging branches. Always keep your tent and pack well away from the flames.
- Fires can quickly get out of control. Make safety your number one priority!
- Keep a bucket of water and a good-sized mound of sand or dirt close by just in case.
- Keep your fire manageable. Although it can be tempting to build a big blaze, that's only going to make it easier to get out of control. Plus a massive inferno is pretty much useless for cooking on.
- Always be sure to put out a fire completely when you're ready to move on. Pour water on the flames and cover the hot sticks with dirt and be sure to stamp out any embers. Never leave a fire burning!

Water

Water is the most precious thing in the world. Even in the best conditions humans can only survive a few days without water — and in hot, dry weather even going a few hours without it can lead to dehydration, fainting and severe illness.

Always make sure you set out with plenty of fresh water but there may be times when you need to find clean water in the wild. Here's how.

Finding and collecting fresh water

Unless you are stranded in the desert or in the ocean, no matter how lost you are, there's a good chance that fresh water will be nearby. All plants and animals need water to survive — and so it can just be a case of finding where they get it from!

Take a good look around and use your senses.
- Can you hear the trickle of a stream?
- Animals always know where the nearest water source is — are there telltale tracks? See p. 54 for more on animal tracks.
- Are you surround by lush green vegetation? This can also be a clue to lots of water nearby.

All rivers and streams have a "source" — that is, a spring, usually in the mountains, where they start. As a general rule, the closer you can get to the source, the fresher / cleaner the water.

Try to avoid still water — such as lakes and ponds. Look instead for fast-running streams because the oxygen created by the movement will make the water cleaner.

SURVIVAL TIP!

Melted snow and ice can be drunk but should be purified — see p. 85. Never eat it frozen: ice lowers your body's temperature and could even make you more dehydrated!

Building a still

An emergency supply of clean water can be collected using what is called a "still". This works by collecting natural condensation, or tiny water droplets, in the air. Be warned, though, it will take a long time to collect a few sips' worth!

1. Stills work best in warm weather — they work even in the desert!

2. Dig a hollow in the ground and place a pan at the bottom.

3. Stretch a plastic sheet tight across the hollow and weigh it down at the ends with stones.

4. Place another large stone in the middle, so that it forms a tight kind of bowl over your pan.

5. As the sun heats up the air, water droplets will condense on the underside of your sheet and drip into the pan.

The water from your still will be pure and ready to drink — as the action of filtering it through your sheet will distil it.

SURVIVAL TIP!
Never drink dirty or saltwater — no matter how thirsty you become. It will make you sick and and actually worsen your dehydration.

Purifying water

As a rule, assume all the water you find in the wild will be dirty. The stuff that comes out of your taps at home has been through an incredible amount of cleaning and purification processes to remove all the natural germs and bacteria that can be found in wild water.

Before you drink any water you collect yourself, you **MUST** purify it! Purification tablets can be bought at most camping shops, but they shouldn't be used too often — besides, the taste is pretty awful!

The best way to purify water is to boil it.

1. First, get rid of any larger bits of sediment or dirt by making a kind of sieve out of a T-shirt and straining the water through it.

2. Then build a good hot fire, pour your strained water into a pot with a lid and get it boiling.

3. Ideally you want it boiling and bubbling away for a steady 10 minutes, before letting it cool.

4. Once it is cool again, it's ready to drink. Enjoy!

Knots – a quick and easy guide to two essential knots

Tying rope or line securely is vital in the wild – and most useful around camp, whether you're building a shelter or simply setting up a clothes line to dry your wet things! Luckily, there is a knot for just about every situation you can think of. A really experienced adventurer will know 20 good strong knots he could tie in the dark ... but, to start with, everyone heading on an expedition should be able to tie these two basic knots.

SURVIVAL TIP!
Practise, practise, practise! Get into the habit of keeping a piece of string in your pocket so you can always have a quick tie and untie whenever you have a spare moment.

Clove hitch
A simple way to fix a line to a solid post.

1. Make a turn around the post with the free end running underneath the standing line.

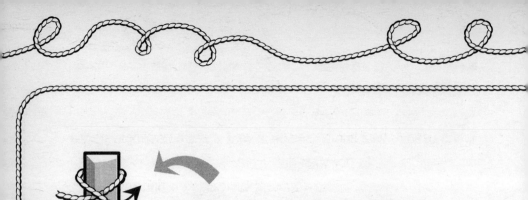

2. Take a second turn in the same direction.

3. Feed the free end through the eye of the second turn.

4. Pull tight.

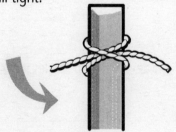

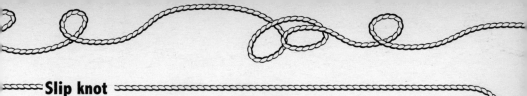

Slip knot

This is used to tie a line to a hook or ring — and is especially useful for fishing.

1. Run your line through the ring and double back so you have two parallel lines of rope.

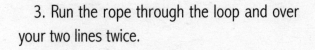

2. Make a loop with your free end.

3. Run the rope through the loop and over your two lines twice.

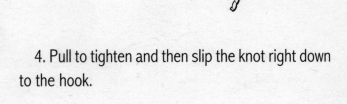

4. Pull to tighten and then slip the knot right down to the hook.

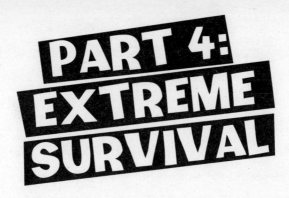

PART 4: EXTREME SURVIVAL

While it's great fun to explore the wilderness near to your house, there comes a time for every true adventurer when he will want to test himself in the toughest conditions the world can throw at him!

Different environments give different challenges to the adventurer. If you're exploring in the desert, you're going to need different skills than if you're trekking through the Antarctic. The following pages should give you a few tips on how to stay healthy and fit in even the most extreme conditions...

Cold

Icy conditions can be as dangerous as very hot weather. If you get too cold, your body will start to "shut down" like a computer processor turning off some programs in order to keep itself going. Eventually, however, the battery will run out altogether — and in your body's case, this is very bad news indeed! This is called "hypothermia" and can be deadly.

The other great danger of the cold is frostbite — when exposed parts of your body get frozen, go black and the cells themselves die. Many unwary — and even experienced — adventurers have lost fingers, toes, and even the tips of their noses through frostbite!

DO: Wrap up properly! Layers of clothes trap heat between each layer, so pile on as much as you can. Wrap a scarf around your face and always keep your hat on.

DON'T: Overdo it. Sweat may seem like a good thing in the cold, but sweat can also freeze — the equivalent of splashing icy water on your face.

DO: Keep moving. Swing your arms, stamp your feet, blow out your cheeks and make faces. Your blood is warm — and you want to keep it flowing to all parts of your body.

DON'T: Sit on cold, wet ground. If you can't find something to use as a stool, then put down leaves, branches or a plastic bag first.

DO: Light a few small fires, rather than one large one. The collected heat from them will be stronger. Use them to heat your food and drink as well as keep you warm.

WARNING!
Hypothermia and frostbite are both deadly conditions brought about by cold. Be sure to recognize the symptoms and how to treat them – see p. 169.

SURVIVAL TIP!
In freezing weather, getting wet is just about the worst thing you can do – the frozen water will make a layer of ice next to your skin. Always change into dry clothes!

TRUE TALE: Scott of the Antarctic

Robert Falcon Scott was a British explorer who is remembered for his tragic attempt to become the first man to reach the South Pole.

In June 1910, Scott's ship, the *Terra Nova* set off from Wales, loaded with supplies including sledges, ponies and dogs. In October he and his team landed in Antarctica with high hopes – but they soon ran into trouble. The weather turned against them and the sledges, ponies and dogs simply couldn't cope. Eventually five men were left to soldier on alone: Scott, Edward Wilson, Henry Bowers, Lawrence Oates and Edgar Evans. It took over a year, but in January 1912, they finally reached the pole – only to find they'd been beaten by a better-prepared and better-equipped Norwegian expedition.

But they still had the terrible trek home: 1,500 km through the worst terrain in the world. They never made it. Evans died in February, and a month later, Oates, crippled by frostbite, told his companions, "I'm just stepping outside. I may be some time". He was never seen again. He sacrificed himself so he wouldn't hold his friends back.

On 29 March 1912, Scott and his last two companions died of frostbite, hypothermia and starvation in their tent. They were only 20 km from a supply depot. Their bodies are still buried there, under a simple monument of snow and ice.

Heat

When you're hot, the body tries to cool itself by sweating – meaning you're losing vital moisture at a much quicker rate than usual so need to drink more water to replace it. Lose too much water and you will become dehydrated, resulting in heatstroke and heat exhaustion.

> ## WARNING!
> **For more advice on dehydration and heatstroke, see p. 171.**

DO: Drink plenty of water. Lots of little sips are better than a few big gulps.

DON'T: Walk in the hottest part of the day (around midday and early afternoon).

DO: Wear loose-fitting, light coloured clothes – they reflect heat.

DON'T: Wear tight, dark clothes – they will absorb heat.

DO: Eat little and often.

DON'T: Eat a large meal – digesting uses lots of vital water!

DO: Keep yourself cool by wiping your face and back of neck with a damp handkerchief.

> **SURVIVAL TIP!**
> Sunburn can be incredibly painful – when it is really hot, avoid the temptation to remove all your clothes, as exposing your skin will only make it worse. Keep your head, neck and shoulders covered and always wear a high factor suncream.

At sea

Exploring the oceans brings its own unique challenges. Setting sail for new and unexplored lands has always made for great adventures – but the high seas have their own dangers…

DO: Take plenty of fresh drinking water and food. Although you may be able to catch fish, you'll have to survive on whatever you take with you.

DON'T: Drink seawater. It's salty and will make you very ill.

DO: Collect rainwater where you can to drink in an emergency.

DON'T: Be tempted to eat and drink whenever you're hungry or thirsty. Ration your supplies to make them last longer.

DO: Keep accurate records of your position, using the sun as a compass and the Pole Star at night (see p. 43).

DON'T: Take risks. Falling overboard can be fatal.

DO: Wear your life jacket all the time!

DON'T: Argue or bicker with your companions. Life at sea means getting along together!

How to survive a shipwreck

1. Try to get as much skin-covering clothes on as possible. Even in tropical waters, the sea can get very cold.

2. Use your life-jacket. This will keep you afloat and help you save energy.

3. If there are lifeboats, move calmly and carefully towards them and wait for your turn.

4. Don't be tempted to jump into the sea chasing a lifeboat. You might get swept away.

5. If there are no lifeboats, look for a floating piece of debris you can use to help keep you stable in the water.

6. Try to get as far away from the sinking ship as possible. When it finally goes under, the suction could pull you with it.

Altitude

Surviving in the mountains means conserving energy and always being aware of any dangers around you.

DO: Wear lots of layers of clothes: the higher you go, the colder it gets. Layers trap heat between them.

DON'T: Skimp when it comes to proper mountain hiking gear. Get the best coat and boots you can afford.

DO: Keep energy levels up with regular bites of chocolate and Kendal Mint Cake.

DON'T: Run, jump or shout unnecessarily. There is less oxygen in the air when you're high — which means it is harder to breathe and you will get tired more easily.

DO: Stay in touch with your companions at all times. Never let one another out of your sight.

DON'T: Go off exploring on your own. Mountains have many hidden dangers!

DO: Tread carefully, keeping an eye out for hidden dangers, such as rockfalls, avalanches and deep crevasses.

DON'T: Ignore weather reports. Mountains are very exposed to the elements, and even small changes in weather can have dangerous consequences.

SURVIVAL TIP!
Altitude sickness
One of the biggest dangers when climbing mountains is altitude sickness. As we go higher, the amount of oxygen we can breathe in decreases – making it difficult for our muscles, organs and brain to work properly. Altitude sickness can be very serious if not treated – see p. 173 for more.

How to survive an avalanche

Avalanches happen when snow on a mountain becomes too heavy, and starts to slip downhill. As it travels it picks up speed until it becomes a massive wall of snow, smashing anything and everything in its way.

Ways to avoid an avalanche

Sometimes there's nothing you can do to stop an avalanche – but you can make sure you don't start one yourself!

1. Stay quiet. Loud noises can set off avalanches!

2. Try to disturb snow as little as possible.

3. Avoid anything which may cause vibrations up the slope that could loosen the snow and start an avalanche.

What to do in the event of an avalanche

1. Secure your hat and gloves and zip up your coat tight. This will stop the snow getting inside your clothes.

2. Just before the snow hits, scream as loud as you can. This will warn others – and let potential rescuers know you're there.

3. When the snow hits, take a deep breath and close your mouth tight.

4. Try to "swim" with the snow.

5. Stay as close to the surface as possible.

6. Try to grab any trees you see as you travel down the mountain. If you can, climb as high as is safe up the tree.

7. As you slow down, keep your hands over your head to protect your face.

8. Wriggle your head around to create breathing space.

9. If you are buried, look for light and try to free your head.

10. Blow your whistle regularly to attract rescuers.

TRUE TALE: Hillary and Tenzing

In 1953, the New Zealand mountaineer Edmund Hillary and his Nepali companion (or "Sherpa") Tenzing Norgay, became the first men to conquer Mount Everest — the tallest mountain in the world.

Many expeditions had tried to climb Everest before, but all had been defeated by the bitter cold, the sudden storms and the sheer scale of the ascent. There's very little oxygen near the top of the mountain, so breathing is difficult, climbers lose energy and the resulting altitude sickness often leads to confusion and even death.

Two men in Hillary and Tenzing's expedition had already turned back when their oxygen supplies failed, but on May 29, Hillary and Tenzing decided to make one final attempt to reach the summit. To get there, they had to climb a treacherous 12 metre rock face. They managed it by wedging themselves between the rock and ice. The rock face is now known as the "Hillary Step" in honour of Hillary.

At 11.30 a.m, Hillary and Tenzing reached the top — both men stepping on to the highest point in the world at the same time.

The news reached the rest of the world on June 2: the day of the Queen's coronation in Britain. The day was already a holiday, but after the papers reported Hillary and Tenzing's achievement, there was double the reason for celebration!

PART 5: HUNTING AND FISHING

Before any expedition into the wild, you should always pack as much food as you can manage — but for really long adventures, there is going to come a time when you need to rely on your own skills to catch your dinner. All of the greatest adventurers were expert hunters or fishermen — and even if you're not planning a long expedition just yet, it can still be great fun to practise their techniques.

But remember — you must never hurt a living animal unnecessarily. And always be very careful when handling fishing hooks or bows and arrows.

Fishing

Fishing is one of the most enjoyable skills you might ever master. From providing an essential source of food on long adventures off the beaten track to a great way to spend an afternoon by your nearest canal, fishing is just about the easiest and quickest way to connect to the wilderness outside your window.

There are a few pointers to remember every time you fish, however, no matter where you are:

• Check if you need a permit to fish on that particular spot. Anyone fishing also has to own a rod licence by law: these can be bought at your local post office.

• Remember that fish are living creatures – and should be treated with respect. Never harm a fish deliberately.

• Keep all your equipment clean and the area you're fishing in tidy. Other animals such as ducks and swans can be badly injured by discarded lines or hooks.

SURVIVAL TIP!
Remember to always be careful around water. Even a fully-grown man can drown in just a few centimetres of water.

How to make your own fishing tackle

Your local fishing tackle shop will sell a dizzying array of fishing gear. While having high quality equipment will always make fishing easier, you really don't need much more than a simple rod, line, hook and bait. And the good news is you can make most of it yourself!

You should carry fishing line and hooks in your pack, but the rest of your tackle can be made for free.

How to make a fishing rod

1. Any strong, supple length of branch will do. It should be flexible enough to bend a bit without snapping, and light enough to lift without much effort ... remember it's going to feel even heavier with a big fish attached to the end!

2. Tie a length of line about two metres long to the end with a good strong knot.

3. Don't make your rod longer than you are tall or it may be difficult to land your fish!

Floats

Floats are the easiest way of telling if a fish has taken your bait. They are attached to the line between your rod and your hook and literally float on the water. When a fish takes a bite out of your bait, it will pull the line – and so pull the float – underwater. If you don't have room to carry floats in your pack, a twig tied to your line can do the job. You don't need to tie a fancy knot – just the knot you use to tie your shoelaces! Make sure it's big enough to spot easily on the water but light enough to dip underwater when you get a bite.

How to make your own float

You can make your own floats using a cork and an elastic band.

1. First, paint the top half of the cork a bright colour that you'll be able to see from the bank.

2. Fix the elastic band tight around the middle.

3. When you rig up your tackle, just pass your line through the elastic band. This will hold the float securely, but means you can also adjust the length of your line too.

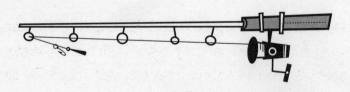

Weight

Weights are used between the float and the hook to make the bait sink lower in the water to where the bigger fish hang out. Professional weight is called "shot" and consists of tiny balls that are simply pinched on to the line – they are very cheap and it is well worth keeping a good supply in your pack.

In a tight spot, however, just about anything that can be tied to your line can be used as improvised weight. The easiest way of doing this is to find a flattish looking rock and secure an elastic band around it – then pass your line through the band like you did with your home-made float.

Finding bait

Every fisherman has a different idea of what bait works best for catching different types of fish. Some swear by the simplest chunk of bread, others spend hours cooking up their own creations and devising recipes a top chef would be proud of. Who knows who's right? The arguments will probably go on for as long as there are fishermen around to debate it.

But in the wild your bait options are limited. Luckily, that doesn't really matter – because of the very simple truth that fish in the wild aren't generally too fussy about what they eat! They'll eat things you might have in your food supplies — bread, cheese and sandwich meat — and some things you probably don't — worms and maggots!

If you want to collect worms, the best time is in the morning, when there's dew on the ground. Keep the worms in a little soil in a sealed container with a few air holes punched in the top.

Know your swim: where to fish for what

Believe it or not, fishing is not simply a case of plonking your bait anywhere in the water and waiting for a bite. Fish tend to hang out at certain spots — and the clever fisherman will know exactly where the best chances of finding them are…

In a river or stream

Outside bends — when a river curves, particles of food tend to move to the outside of the bend, so that's where you'll find the fish. If there's also a rock or fallen tree to slow down the current then you've an even better chance!

Behind rocks — a big rock or other obstacle in a river will create a natural pocket of clear, calm water behind it. Fish will often use these pockets to rest from battling the current.

Where two streams meet — faster currents carry more food, and any joining of two streams will provide a feeding ground for fish.

Overhanging trees and branches — these provide shade and rest for the fish, as well as protection from birds. Bigger fish can often be found lurking here — but don't get your line tangled on the branches. Your tackle is precious and you don't want to lose any of it!

In a lake

Sloping cliffs — cliffs that drop straight down into deep water tend not to attract fish, but gently-sloping food can hold up food for them.

Weed beds and lily pads — these are fantastic places to find fish as they provide plenty of food and shelter. Insects attract little fish, and the little fish attract bigger fish! Reeds are also terrible tangling spots, however — so be extra careful not to lose any precious tackle!

Jetties and moorings — the "legs" of any kind of structure attract plants, smaller creatures, and the fish that like to feed on them.

Fishing tips and tricks

The first and most important lesson you have to learn about fishing is patience! The old hunter's saying goes: if fishing were just about catching, it wouldn't be called fishing — it would be called catching!

There are, however, a few handy tricks to help you get a little more success on the riverbank…

- Always look for where the water goes from shallow to deep — that's where the fish tend to get together to look for food.

- You don't have to try to cast out right into the middle of the river — you'll actually get more bites closer to the shoreline.

- Try to fish as close to the bottom as you can — that's where the bigger catches are.

- Sunrise is a brilliant time to fish. Get up early and cast off!

- Watch your line and float carefully. Learn the difference between a fish that's just investigating your bait, and one that's really biting.

- Bait is important. If one bait isn't working, forget it and try something else.

- Practise casting. And then practise some more! A really good fisherman can pop his bait down in the same spot every time.

- When fishing in rivers, cast upstream and let your bait move downstream with the current. This will make it look more natural to the fish than if it was just hanging there in the water.

Sea fishing

Fishing in the sea brings its own challenges and rewards. While some of the principles remain the same, the sheer size of the ocean means learning some new skills.

Spinners

The sea is generally too deep and choppy to fish using floats, so the best method is to use a "spinner". These are special hooks that come attached to shiny, metal "fish". The idea is that as the spinner travels through the water, it looks like a little fish – tempting bigger fish to take a bite!

How to spin

1. Tie a spinner – along with a weight – to the end of your line using the same knot as you would for a hook (see p. 89).

2. Cast off as far into the water as you can.

3. Let the line run out a good distance, so your spinner sinks deep into the sea.

4. Slowly reel the line back in, feeling all the time for the tug on the line which means a fish has taken the bait.

5. If you don't get a bite, cast off and try again!

Other bait

Some sea fishermen prefer to use chunks of real fish rather than spinners – as the smell attracts other fish. Simply put a chunk of the fish on to your hook and cast off just as you would with a spinner.

SURVIVAL TIP!
It's worth having a look for fish in rock pools – natural pools found between rocks on the seashore at low tide. Often these pools are hidden underwater at high tide, then as the tide goes out, some fish get trapped in them.

TRUE TALE: The Kon-Tiki Expedition

On 28 April 1947, six men in a raft made of balsa wood were towed out of Callao harbour in Peru and left adrift in the Pacific Ocean. 101 days later, after an incredible journey of 4,300 miles across the world's largest ocean, they washed up safely in Polynesia. The raft was called the *Kon-Tiki*, and the expedition is remembered as one of the most amazing sea journeys of all time.

Leading the expedition was the Norwegian Thor Heyerdahl. He wanted to find out whether the Incas of Peru could have explored the islands in the Pacific. His raft was a copy of the earliest found in South America and was made mostly of super-lightweight balsa wood. Heyerdahl's team had some modern radio equipment, but they had to rely on the ancient design of the boat for seaworthiness.

The crew had just one sail for power, but still managed to keep a steady course west. They collected and rationed rainwater, and became expert fishermen. Once they were almost capsized by the world's largest fish, a whale shark, but the balsa wood was so buoyant they managed to stay afloat. It's thought a more modern boat, made from steel, wouldn't have survived.

After the *Kon-Tiki* washed up, the raft was shipped back to Norway – you can still visit it today in a museum on the outskirts of Oslo.

Hunting and foraging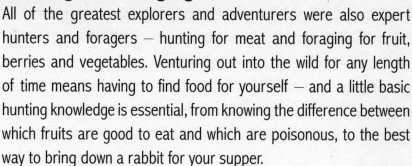

All of the greatest explorers and adventurers were also expert hunters and foragers – hunting for meat and foraging for fruit, berries and vegetables. Venturing out into the wild for any length of time means having to find food for yourself – and a little basic hunting knowledge is essential, from knowing the difference between which fruits are good to eat and which are poisonous, to the best way to bring down a rabbit for your supper.

However, there are strict rules and laws concerning hunting any animals – and you must find out exactly what the law is in the area you plan to explore before you leave. The golden rule is that you should never try to kill any animal in the wild for sport – and only for food if it's absolutely essential for your survival. It's best to think of the following techniques as purely theoretical for now… Practise them in your garden – but be careful **NEVER** to aim at another person!

Bows and arrows

Before the invention of guns, the bow and arrow was the best, most effective and deadliest weapon in any hunter's armoury. For centuries our ancestors have relied on the bow and arrow for hunting food. Part of its appeal is that making your own bow and arrow is actually pretty simple. Try following the steps below – but remember that even the most basic bow and arrow can cause serious damage and injury. Remember, **NEVER** aim at another person or animal!

How to make your own bow and arrow

1. First, find a good length of wood – ideally about as long as from your feet to your waist.

2. Never snap off a branch from a tree – look instead for fallen wood, but make sure it is not too dry or cracked. Yew trees make excellent wood for bows.

3. Your bow should be flexible enough to have some bend, but strong enough to snap back into place.

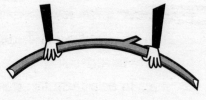

4. Shape the bow by whittling with your penknife until the middle is thicker than the ends. Be careful to shave the wood gently, and only from the inside of what will be the curve of the bow.

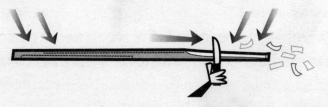

5. Use your knife to cut notches for the string, about an inch from each end of the bow.

6. The simplest string to use is your fishing line. Cut a length a little less than the length of your bow and tie it tight at each end.

7. You want the bow to have a gentle permanent bend — remember to allow yourself enough room for the bow to bend back further when you fire an arrow.

8. Arrows can be made from strong, straight sticks of dry, dead wood. They should be about a third of the length of your bow.

9. To help them fly straighter, try lashing feathers to the end. The best way to do this is to score a groove in the arrow, slide the feather in as much as possible and secure it by wrapping in thin thread.

10. Sharpen the business end of your arrow very carefully with your knife — but remember never to fire it at another living thing!

How to fire a bow and arrow

Don't expect to be Robin Hood straight away. It will take time and practice to shoot arrows accurately.

1. With the string slack, hold the bow in the middle but pointed downwards — as if you're firing into the ground.

2. Grip it with your weaker hand (i.e. your left hand if you are right-handed).

3. Select an arrow and hold it at the back end between your first and second fingers. Use your thumb to keep it steady.

4. Fit the arrow to the string, keeping the bow pointed down and the arrow straight at a 90 degree angle to the bow.

5. Using your bow-holding hand as a kind of rest, slowly draw the arrow back towards you, all the while keeping the bow pointed downwards.

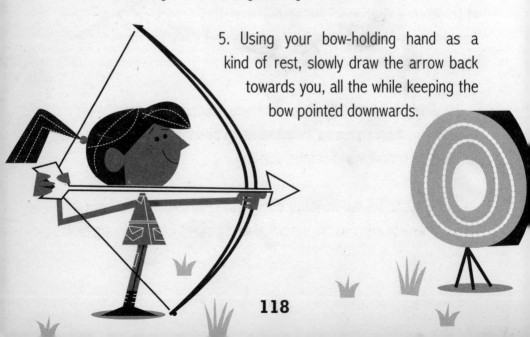

6. When the string is tight and the bow is bending, carefully raise the bow and sight along the arrow until it is pointing at your target.

7. Release the string as smoothly as you can – and keep your bow perfectly still until the arrow has hit the target.

Targets and techniques

You can have the best equipment in the world – but if you can't use it properly then it's basically useless … but of course, with a little practice, even the most basic and improvised bow and arrow can be used with a fair amount of accuracy.

Make a target

Find a good clear area in which to practise. Don't just concentrate on the narrow "corridor" between you and the target – make sure there is plenty of space to the sides and behind too. You never know when a throw or a shot might go wild!

Find the biggest slab of wood or stone you can to use as your target. Prop it up against a tree and use a piece of chalk to draw a bullseye, with more rings on the outside.

Don't expect to hit the bullseye every time! For a little while you'll be doing well to even hit the target at all, so don't get discouraged.

Responsibility and the law

Hunting is a very tightly regulated sport and you must be fully aware of all the local laws concerning what you can and can't do.

Never hurt an animal unnecessarily. It is not only cruel, but illegal. You should only ever hunt for animals if your life depends upon it. Being a good adventurer means having respect for nature — and that includes all animals.

Be extremely careful when handling any weapon. Never point them at another person.

Make sure you always have your first-aid kit with you, and know how to use it (see p. 162).

Wild berries and fruit

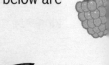

Be careful with any wild fruit or berries — remember that if you're in any doubt at all, don't eat it. All of the fruit and berries below are easy to spot, fairly widespread and taste delicious…

Apples and pears

These grow in the wild – and are if anything even tastier than the kind you find in the supermarket! Watch out for small "crab" apples – and never eat unripe apples as they can give you a nasty stomach ache.

Wild strawberries

Found on hillsides and woodlands in late spring and summer all around the world. The flavour tends to be more intense than the kind you're used to.

Blackberries

The most common wild berry in the British countryside — and found throughout the summer across the whole of the Northern Hemisphere and in South America.

Raspberries

Also surprisingly common in the wild, these make for a wonderful snack on the move — or a tasty treat for dessert. They can be found from late spring throughout the summer in Europe and North America.

Oranges

In hot temperate climates, such as the Mediterranean, Brazil, Mexico and parts of North America, oranges grow plentifully in the wild — and are delicious in summer plucked straight from the tree!

TRUE TALE: Burke and Wills

In 1860, the Australian government offered a huge prize to the first explorers to cross the continent from south to north. Australia was mostly desert, and only the Aborigines, who'd lived there for thousands of years, knew how to live in the outback. But when, on 20 August, Robert Burke and William Wills took up the government's challenge, they didn't seek the help of Aborigine guides.

The expedition stalled at a place called Cooper Creek, and Burke, Wills and two other men, Charles Gray and John King, carried on alone. They told the others to wait for their return. After two months they reached the north coast – they'd made it against all the odds.

But now they had to get back. On the gruelling return journey, Gray fell ill and died. Burke decided to stop and bury him – a fatal mistake. When, exhausted and starving, Burke, Wills and King made it back to Cooper Creek, they found the rest of the party had set off just nine hours earlier. The time they'd spent burying Gray cost Burke and Wills their lives, and they both died of starvation in July 1861.

The last man, King, was nursed back to health by the Aborigines until he was rescued. He brought the bones of Burke and Wills back to Melbourne with him, and they were given the biggest public funeral the city had ever held.

Poison!

The golden rule with all fruit, berries and plants in the wild is to assume that they're poisonous. If you're not absolutely sure about anything, don't eat it! Just because you've seen an animal eating something, that doesn't mean it's OK for you to eat. Our bodies work differently and many foods that are OK for

animals are deadly poisonous to us. Just look at cows – if we ate grass, our bodies wouldn't be able to digest it and we would end up very sick!

The best way to learn which plants are poisonous and which are safe is to go on an expedition with an experienced adult. There's no substitute for being shown first hand what's good and what to avoid. This is just a small selection of some of the most common poisonous plants – never eat anything unless you're absolutely sure about it!

Laburnum

All parts of this tree are poisonous. Symptoms include headache, stomach ache and a burning throat. It grows throughout southern Europe and can be easily spotted by its distinctive bright yellow flowers that hang from the branches.

Foxglove

The whole plant is poisonous and will give you stomach ache, headache, sleepiness, dizziness and sickness. You can spot it very easily – the plants grow very straight and have lots of purple bell-shaped flowers. It grows throughout Europe, west and central Asia and north-west Africa.

Poison ivy

This plant is mostly found in North America and is poisonous to even touch! The leaves grow in threes and are almond-shaped, and the plants are often found growing up trees like vines, and occasionally as shrubs themselves, with greyish-white berries. Just brushing against it will bring you out in blisters and a painful rash. The poison can also be carried in smoke, so be careful not to burn it either.

Hemlock

All of this white plant is very bad for you – and will make you too weak to move ... except to be sick. It grows all over the world and the lacy-looking leaves make triangle shapes with clusters of white flowers about 10 cm across.

SURVIVAL TIP!

If you think you or one of your companions have eaten something poisonous then get medical help immediately. Try to keep some of the berries or leaves to show the doctors. And remember – there are plenty more poisonous plants out there – so unless you're absolutely sure something's safe, never put it near your mouth!

Mushrooms

Never eat any mushrooms or toadstools in the wild. It takes years of studying to spot the small differences between edible and poisonous mushrooms – get it wrong and the effects can be terrible. See some of the worst offenders below.

The cap mushroom

Appearance: A bulbous sheath at the bottom, with white gills and stalk and a dirty white or green cap.

Effects: Sickness, huge pain, diarrhoea, coma, occasionally even death.

Fly agaric

Appearance: White stalk and gills with a red cap with white spots or "warts" on it.

Effects: Sickness, dizziness, hallucinations.

Livid entoloma

Appearance: Yellow or pinkish gills and a yellowy-grey cap.

Effects: Sickness, weakness, diarrhoea, pain.

PART 6: CAMPFIRE COOKERY

If you're going to last more than a few hours in the wild, you're going to have to learn how to cook. There are no microwave ovens, takeaways or pizza delivery services out here!

Luckily, campfire cooking is great fun – and the shared experience of all mucking in together, before enjoying a hearty meal you've prepared yourself, eaten in the fresh air, can be one of the best things about any expedition.

You don't even need to be a great cook – just as long as you've got a couple of recipes up your sleeve and know what you're doing around a campfire, you should be able to make some delicious dinners. And of course everything tastes better when it's cooked on a campfire!

Supplies

With space in your backpack limited, you obviously don't want to be carting loads of ingredients as well as half your mum's crockery around with you! A few basics used cleverly can provide all you need — most campfire meals are cooked out of one or two pans anyway … and if you're really smart you can even eat out of the same pan you cooked with.

Food

Always try to find room in your pack for a few staples that can provide easy-to-cook, nourishing food in almost any situation where you can get a fire going.

Pasta/rice

Get the easy cook kind. All you'll have to do is boil for around 10 minutes.

Potatoes

Spuds are brilliant for boiling or cooking in their jackets … and will keep for days. Stuff a few good big ones where you can!

Beans

Baked beans have been the campers' favourite since the days of the Wild West!

Sausages

Sausages are great for frying. In very hot weather these won't keep beyond a day, so be sure to eat them early on in your expedition.

Bacon

Just as with the sausages, bacon won't keep too long in the warm. The advantage of bacon is you can pack more of it.

Tomato sauce

A couple of jars of tomato sauce will improve any pasta or rice dish!

Eggs

A wonderful cooking staple for fry-ups and omelettes, you'll have to be very careful how you pack them. You DO NOT want smashed egg all over your gear! A good trick is to hard boil a few before you set out, for a tasty treat that can be eaten on the march. It is best to eat them the same day you boil them.

SURVIVAL TIP!

Rather than lug around all the bulky packaging your supplies came in, repackage food into airtight ziplock bags before your trip. This not only saves space and weight but cuts down on waste.

Cooking equipment

The really smart adventurer only needs the bare minimum of pots and pans with him in the wild. Camping shops sell clever sets that fold into each other to save space and it is well worth looking into these … but in the meantime, just concentrate on the following.

Billy can

This is the most useful multi-purpose item in the camp kitchen! Basically a saucepan, a billy can cook just about anything – and can even be used for heating water to make your morning cup of tea! It also doubles up as a serving vessel – meaning you cook and eat out of the same pot. Less washing up!

Frying pan

While you can fry sausages, bacon and eggs in a billy, it is definitely easier in a frying pan. Make sure it has a metal handle and high sides.

SURVIVAL TIP!

If you have a spare billy, fill it full of water and set it heating as you eat. By the time you've finished dinner, you'll have hot water for washing up!

Cooking tips

Frying: you can sit your frying pan directly onto hot coals, being careful that no flames lick over the sides. Always be careful to keep the handle pointed out of the fire, and never touch the pan (or the handle) without a towel or cloth wrapped around your hand to protect it.

Billies

Although you can sit your billy directly on to hot coals, when boiling water for pasta or rice, a better and safer technique is to hang the pot above the flames. See below for how to build your own tripod in the wild.

Tinfoil

Lots of things can be cooked by simply wrapping them in a double layer of tinfoil with the shiny side in and placing them on hot coals. Check the food to make sure it's not getting too burnt, but rough cooking times are below:

Potatoes: 1 hour
Whole fish: 20 minutes
Sausages: 30 minutes
Whole apples: 30 minutes

How to make a cooking tripod

You will need:

- Three straight sticks about a metre long
- String
- Your knife

1. With your knife, carefully strip the bark away from your sticks and sharpen one end of each of them into a point.

2. Soak your sticks in a stream for an hour so they don't catch fire!

3. Push the sharpened ends of two of the sticks into the ground on each side of your fire, so they cross to form a V about 10 cm from the top.

4. Tie the two sticks together using an "over and under" technique with your string.

5. Push your third stick into the ground so it rests into the V you've made from the first two sticks — and tie it to the others using the same technique.

6. Now your tripod is ready! Simply tie some rope around the handle of your pan and lift it to the desired height (just above the flames is best). Then wrap the end of the rope round and round your V at the top of your tripod until it is secure.

Recipes

Before you leave on an expedition you should make sure you know how to cook simple recipes such as boiled pasta or rice – and experiment with adding them to tomato sauce to make an easy and filling meal. These will always give you a good solid nutritious dinner … but after a while can get a little boring. Try spicing up your mealtimes with the following easy recipes:

Classic Camp Fry Up

Ingredients:

Sausages

Bacon

Eggs

Beans

1. Prick your sausages and fry in your frying pan over hot coals, turning every now and then to make sure they brown evenly.

2. After 10 minutes or so, add the bacon.

3. In a separate billy, get your beans heating gently.

4. When it's all nearly ready (about another ten minutes), crack open an egg or two into your frying pan and cook the lot for another five minutes.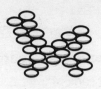

5. Don't worry about your sausages, bacon and eggs getting all mixed up in the pan — some say they taste better that way!

Hungry Hamburgers

Ingredients:

Hamburgers

Vegetables – try sliced onions and peppers

Buns

1. Place each hamburger in a double-wrapped foil parcel.

2. Then put the sliced onions, peppers and whatever other veg you fancy on top of the hamburger.

3. Wrap it all up in the foil, making sure there are no tears or holes.

4. Cook on top of hot coals in the fire for about 20-25 minutes.

5. When they're ready, tip it all into a bun and tuck in!

Ultimate Pitta Pizzas

Ingredients:

Pitta bread
Tomato paste
Margarine or butter
Mushrooms
Grated cheese
Sliced onion
Sliced pepper

1. Make a makeshift grille over your fire using whatever is to hand — wire mesh works well (camping or barbecue grilles can be bought cheaply).

2. Cover your pitta with sauce, add the mushrooms, onion and pepper and then sprinkle loads of cheese on top.

3. Carefully fold in half and spread margarine or butter over one side.

4. Place that side down on the grille and cook until golden brown.

5. Now carefully spreading marge or butter on the other half and flip over.

6. When that side is golden too, they're ready to eat!

Storing food

Storing your food carefully is very important. Obviously because you don't want to lose it, have it get spoiled or go off – but also because any food will attract hungry wild animals. And whether the creatures are as big as bears or as small as ants, you don't want anything coming after your dinner!

• Never leave food in your tent. Not only will it leave your tent with the lingering smell of raw food, the aroma may still attract bears even after you've removed the food itself.

• For the same reason, try not to leave food in your pack. A hungry animal will chew right through your rucksack to get to a tasty snack.

• Keep raw meat separate from everything else. And always wash your hands after handling raw meat – with soap and hot water if at all possible.

• Cook a good distance from your sleeping area if possible. No matter how careful you are, some food is always going to get dropped – and the last thing you want is to attract a column of ants or a swarm of flies right next to your sleeping bag.

• Tidy as you go. It will make clearing up afterwards much easier, and you'll be less likely to make a mess.

• Hang your food from a bag slung over the branch of a tree well away from your tent. This is essential in bear country.

Hygiene

You must be careful to keep everything related to preparing and eating food as clean as you can. Believe it or not, you've got more chance of making yourself ill when you're cooking or eating than at any other time when out in the wild.

• Always wash your hands before cooking – and again before eating. Give them another wash every time you handle raw meat.

• Use hot water and soap to wash. If you can't heat up water, then fast-moving running water is next best.

• Try not to spill bits of food and tidy up any crumbs – they will attract wild animals and insects.

• Keep your raw food in airtight containers as much as possible. This will help them last longer before going off.

• Always make sure meat is thoroughly cooked through before eating – and that it is piping hot in the middle. If in doubt, it's far better to eat something that's a little bit overdone than it is to take a chance with something that might still be raw.

PART 7: SURVIVING IN THE WILD

We are not alone in the wild. There may not be many people around, but the wild is teeming with an amazing abundance of animal and plant life. Some of it is useful, some tasty ... and some you'll want to try your best to avoid!

The real adventurer knows how to share the wild with all this life – not dominating or controlling it, but to live in harmony with it, and harness it to make the best use of everything that nature's providing.

TRUE TALE: Daniel Boone

Boone was one of America's first heroes — a soldier, a hunter, and a pioneer of the new land. There are so many tales told of his exploits that it can be hard to know what's true and what's legend.

Boone was born in 1734 on the Pennsylvania frontier: right at the edge of the wild. He grew up to become a great hunter, disappearing into the Blue Ridge Mountains for months at a time chasing down deer, beavers and otters — for food and for their skins, which were used to make clothes. He became famous for being able to find and follow trails other men couldn't see.

In America at that time, there was trouble between the European settlers and the American Indian tribesmen. But over time, a mutual respect built up between Boone and the local chiefs. They recognized each other as true lovers of the wild.

When the Shawnee tribe attacked the town of Boonesborough, Boone persuaded the people to surrender peacefully. The chief of the tribe was so impressed, he made Boone an honorary member of the tribe, and gave him the name "Sheltowee", meaning "Big Turtle". It was the greatest honour the American Indians could bestow on a white settler — and helped cement Boone's reputation. His adventures were the inspiration for the book *Last of the Mohicans*.

Dangerous animals

Most animals are not aggressive to man by nature — but that doesn't mean that they are safe. A wild animal is just that: wild. And if they feel threatened, or afraid, or think that you might be a danger to their young, then things can turn nasty very quickly. This is true of all animals — even pets such as cats and dogs ... but a frightened, threatened bear defending its cubs is a totally different prospect to an angry tabby cat at home!

The best advice anyone can give you concerning dangerous animals is simply to keep your wits about you. Stay alert — use all your senses. If you think you may be too close to a dangerous animal then get away as quickly and as calmly as you can.

Mating season

Many normally gentle animals become very aggressive during mating season, when they are trying to impress their mates with their strength and courage. Don't just assume that mating season is always spring — deer, for example, mate in the autumn, and normally placid stags become ferocious beasts.

Make sure you are aware of all the animals that you are likely to come across in an area before you start to explore. This will not only make your adventure more enjoyable as you spot the different animals, it will also make you aware of any dangers you may encounter.

Young animals

If you should come across a baby animal, don't be tempted to pet it, or even approach it, no matter how cute it looks. The baby itself may not be a threat — but its mother certainly will be! No parent strays very far from their young ... and all will attack if they think their baby is in danger.

Feeding

Never feed wild animals. It not only risks poisoning them with something their stomachs can't cope with, but it might also attract larger, more dangerous animals looking for a bit of free food too.

Statistics:

Black and grizzly bears: average 30 attacks (2 fatal) per year
Sharks: average 60 attacks (4 fatal) per year
Tigers: average 150 attacks (100 fatal) per year

Survive a bear attack

Bears are just about the most dangerous animal you're likely to meet in the wild: in parts of North America, encounters with grizzly and black bears are actually quite common!

The best way to survive a bear attack is not to be around bears in the first place! But if you should find yourself confronted with a huge angry bear, it's worth bearing the following in mind.

The first thing is to spot exactly what kind of bear it is — as you'll see from the advice below, this is crucial! Grizzly bears are around six feet tall, with brown hair, massive long claws and a distinctive shoulder hump. Black bears are slightly smaller, without the hump or the long claws — and can, believe it or not, be blond as well as black.

Survive a grizzly attack

1. Don't run! If you leg it, the bear will simply assume it's because you're worth chasing. Also, as grizzlies can sprint at 30 mph, not even Usain Bolt would have much of a chance of outpacing one...

2. Drop to the ground – and wrap your arms around your head. Curl up and make yourself as small and not-worth-bothering-with as possible.

3. Play dead. Grizzlies only attack when they feel threatened. Once it thinks you're finished, most bears will wander off. Be careful though – don't get up immediately … some cunning bears will hang around just out of sight to see if you miraculously come back to life!

Survive a black bear attack

Black bears are a little different in temperament to grizzlies – and so handling them means acting a little bit differently.

1. Stand your ground – and make lots of noise. Black bears often bluff it when attacking. If it thinks you might put up a fight it could back off.

2. Don't climb a tree. Black bears are expert tree climbers!

3. Fight back. It sounds crazy, but you should lay into the bear with everything you've got. Play dirty – and aim for the face and snout especially. Like all bullies, if a black bear thinks you might do it some damage back, it will often turn and run away itself.

TRUE TALE: Davy Crockett

Davy Crockett was born in 1787 in Tennessee. Aged 12, he became a cowboy, herding cattle across vast plains. But cowboy life didn't suit him. At 13 he ran away to live in the wild all by himself.

Crockett built up a fearsome reputation as a hunter and expert man of the woods. Tales were told of his eerie ability to find and follow a trail, of his strength and cunning in a fight, and of his courage even in the face of extreme danger.

He was most famous for tracking and killing black and grizzly bears. One fight with a black bear nearly finished him off. Crockett fought the bear all night, using a long pole to jab and punch, and ducking out of the way of its deadly paws. After finally defeating the bear, he was so cold and exhausted he feared he'd die in the night — so he spent the hours before daylight shinning up and down a tall tree to keep warm and stay alert.

He became so well-known that he gave up life in the wild and became a successful politician — but he was never really happy with city life. Before long he'd put on his old racoon skin hat and escaped back into the wild. He died as one of the most famous men in the Wild West, fighting at the Battle of Alamo in Texas in 1836.

Survive a shark attack

Despite films like Jaws, it's pretty rare to be attacked by a shark. However, if you do find yourself swimming in shark-infested waters it's worth knowing what to do!

1. The first rule sounds silly, but it makes sense when you think about it: sharks eat fish, so the most important thing is to make yourself look as different to a fish as you can! Shiny watches, jewellery and bright swimming trunks can all fool a hungry Great White into thinking you're dinner...

2. The next thing to remember is to stay away from spots where sharks might be feeding — look out for groups of birds swooping and diving into the water. This is a sign of a shoal of fish and usually means something bigger is hunting there too.

3. If you cut yourself, try to get out of the water as soon as you can. If you can't get out, at least try to stop the bleeding or keep the cut out of the water. Sharks can smell blood from miles away.

If you are attacked...

1. Don't thrash around in panic. Your wild, uncoordinated movements will look to a shark like you're injured – and an easy kill.

2. Stay calm and wait for your moment. When you can, hit it as hard as you can with whatever you've got.

3. Aim for the face – the eyes and nose especially. Believe it or not, giving a shark a black eye can actually send it swimming away shamefaced! In 2010, 14-year-old Lydia Ward was attacked by a five-foot long shark in New Zealand. She fought it off by whacking it in the face with her bodyboard!

Survive a piranha attack

Piranhas live in the rivers of the South American jungles — and are just about the scariest thing you'll ever hear of in the water. Although they're not very big (about 14 to 26 cm long), they're super fast and come armed with rows of razor-sharp teeth … and plenty of bad attitude. To make matters worse, piranhas hunt in huge shoals that can contain hundreds of the angry fish.

A piranha attack can be devastating. Animals the size of goats have been stripped down to bones in just minutes — meaning that if you are attacked, you basically have no chance. However: if you should find yourself having to cross a piranha-infested river, the smart adventurer can take a few steps to avoid an attack in the first place…

1. Wait until dark. Although it may seem scarier that way, piranhas do have to sleep and you have more chance while they're all napping.

2. Don't cross in a dry spell. No rain can mean the river drying up — and less food for the piranhas. If they're hungry they're going to be much more keen to go for anything setting foot in the water.

3. Pick a fast moving spot to cross. Piranhas hang out where the water is more still and warmer.

4. If you can, distract any potential piranhas by throwing some food for them downstream of your crossing spot. It will have to be meat, however – and there will have to be a lot of it!

5. If you can possibly avoid it, don't cross piranha-infested waters when you're bleeding or have an open wound. The piranhas will sense the blood and come looking for you!

Survive a lion attack

Lions still see humans as a threat to food, and so are very dangerous! If a lion does attack you, your chances of survival are not brilliant – but there are some precautions you can take to avoid being attacked in the first place … and if you are attacked, there are some techniques that might just mean the difference between life and death.

Lion caution

1. Never approach a lion – and steer well clear of lionesses with cubs.

2. Male lions are especially aggressive during courtship, when they're trying to impress potential mates.

3. Be especially careful at night. Lions love to hunt when the sun has gone down!

If you are attacked by a lion...

1. Try not to be too frightened! You will need your wits about you!

2. Don't run — if a charging lion sees you flee, he will certainly think you're worth attacking.

3. Stand your ground. Look the lion straight in the eye.

4. Clap your hands, shout and wave your arms about to make yourself look bigger.

5. Never turn your back on the lion. With any luck he'll think you're too much bother and will eventually slink away.

Venomous nasties

It is not just the big beasts you have to worry about — the wild is teeming with tiny animals that can cause a whole lot of pain. Some you'll already know about — bees and wasps, for example — and others are more rare ... and more deadly.

The rules for dealing with stinging and biting insects are the same, however. Keep your eyes peeled for them ... and if you can, leave well alone if you find them.

There are a few more precautions you can take...

DO: Keep your shoes and thick socks on whenever possible.

DON'T: Put your hands anywhere you haven't checked first — such as in holes or crevices, under stones or behind logs.

DO: Walk noisily. If you scare them off in the first place, they can't hurt you.

DON'T: Get into your sleeping bag without shaking it out first. You never know what might be taking a nap in there!

DO: Check all clothes and shoes before putting them on.

How to survive a bee swarm

Bees swarm to protect their hive — and when they do they can be very dangerous. Huge amounts of them will attack together.

1. Never approach a beehive — you'll only make them angry!

2. If you see a swarm, get away from it as fast as possible.

3. The bees may chase you until they think you're no longer a threat, so you might have to run a fair distance.

4. Aim for long grass as this will give you some cover.

5. Water is no good — they will just wait for you to surface before stinging.

6. Try not to swat at them — it's just going to make them more angry!

Killer creepy-crawlies

You'll be very unlucky to come across one of these little critters … but if you do, seek emergency medical help – all of them can be deadly.

Scorpions

They live in sandy or rocky areas and stone walls and can be spotted by their distinctive stinging tail.

Black widow spider

These small spiders can be spotted by their bulbous abdomen — marked with a red hourglass shape or two red spots. They are found in every continent of the world except Antarctica.

Mosquito

These are deadly fly-like creatures that suck blood — and so are responsible for passing disease. Although they are tiny, the diseases they spread kill millions a year.

Poisonous snakes

Leave snakes alone — and don't whatever you do try to capture or kill them. All snakes are afraid of us and they're going to want to escape rather than have to fight.

That said, when they do fight, they usually win! Here's a few of the nastiest to avoid…

Adder

Adders are found throughout Europe and Asia. They grow to between 60 and 90 cm long and most species can be recognized by the dark zigzag pattern down their backs.

Rattlesnake

They are native to North and South America and can be recognized by their distinctive "rattle" on the tip of their tail — the rattling noise acts as a warning they are about to strike!

Cobra

These snakes are found in Africa and Asia and are recognizable by their habit of "standing up" before they strike — as well as flattening their necks like a collar.

How to deal with snake poison

If you are bitten by a poisonous snake, don't panic. Remaining calm is the most important thing you can do to increase your chances of survival – even if you're unlucky enough to be attacked by one of the deadliest snakes.

1. Identify the snake. If you recognize the snake, make a note of it. If not, scribble down any markings it has – this information can be vital once you get to a hospital.

2. Write down the snake's size and the time you were bitten.

3. Get help! Even if the bite doesn't hurt much straight away, you need to find a doctor as soon as possible – especially if the skin around the bite changes colour or starts to swell.

4. Remove anything that might start to pinch with swelling – this includes watches, any bracelets, necklaces or even tight clothing.

5. Keep the bitten area lower than your heart – this will stop the poison spreading too quickly.

6. Bandage the area – though not too tightly. You want to slow the poison down, not cut off the blood flow completely.

PART 8: FIRST AID AND EMERGENCIES

The wild is not a safe place. That's what makes it so exciting – but it also makes every adventure potentially dangerous. No matter how careful you are, accidents and emergencies do happen. And when they do, you should know how to deal with them.

The following pages should not be treated as a complete guide to coping in an emergency – a good adventurer will be sure to take a course in first aid, given by a professional. Try asking at your school, scouts or youth club.

First-aid kit

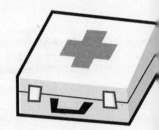

Whenever you go into the wild — even if it's for a very short trip — you should always take your first-aid kit with you. Hopefully you won't need to use it — but if you ever should, you'll be glad you did remember it!

A basic first-aid kit should contain the following items, keep them clean and sealed in plastic bags. Your kit itself should all fit into a waterproof box with a tight-fitting lid — ice cream boxes are ideal.

Pack of plasters – assorted sizes

Use these for treating small cuts and grazes (see p. 169).

Roll of cotton bandage

Ideal for larger wounds when a plaster is too small.

Larger triangular bandage

For making a sling (see p. 174).

Suntan lotion

To protect against sunburn — always a good idea to put some one just in case, even if it doesn't seem too sunny.

Calamine lotion

Great for soothing stings and sunburn.

Cotton wool

For cleaning wounds before applying plasters and bandages.

Scissors

For cutting bandages.

Safety pins

For making a sling and ideal if you something breaks and you don't have time to stitch it back together.

Chocolate

Chocolate is perfect for treating shock and supplying a quick energy hit.

Antiseptic wipes

For sterilizing hands and wounds.

First steps

First aid is the name given to the first steps we take to help someone who is hurt or injured before professional help arrives. It is not a substitute for proper treatment — but it is important. Without first aid even the simplest cuts and bumps could develop into something more serious — and in extreme cases, knowing first aid could even save someone's life.

After any accident, always look around to make sure that any danger has passed. You won't be any help to anyone if you end up getting injured yourself!

Once you're happy that it's safe to treat your patient, there are three things you should always check. The order is easy to remember: just think A, B, C.

1. Airways. Check that the airways — nose and mouth — are clear. Gently tilt the patient's head back so their tongue is not in the way of their air passage.

2. Breathing. Is the patient breathing? Carefully place your head very close to their mouth. Can you feel breath?

3. Circulation. Check that the patient's heart is beating. The easiest way to take someone's pulse is to place two fingers gently but firmly next to their Adam's apple.

After you've checked these three things and they are all OK, you can get on with treating any smaller injuries.

How to give CPR

CPR stands for cardiopulmonary resuscitation – which is a medical term for reviving someone who is unconscious and not breathing. It is an emergency technique and before using it, you **MUST** remember the following!

- **NEVER** practise CPR on a healthy person.
- **ALWAYS** make sure you have attended a proper course given by a trained professional before you attempt CPR. Getting it wrong can do more damage.

If you do need to give CPR, however, the basics are below.

1. Clear the patient's mouth – including sick, blood or other objects. Tilt the head back with the chin pushed up to clear the airways.

2. Check again to see if the patient is breathing. If he is, put him in the recovery position.

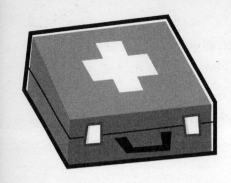

3. If he's still not breathing, place your hands on the patient's chest and press down with the heel of your hand at a steady rate of about once a second. Do this 30 times.

4. If he's still not breathing, open his mouth with one hand and pinch his nostrils together with the other. Take a deep breath, cover his mouth with yours and blow deeply for about one second. Do this twice.

5. Keep repeating the chest compressions and rescue breaths until he starts to breathe or help arrives.

Treating burns

Even small burns can be very painful – and larger burns can be very serious. It's important never to apply ointment to burns and only very small burns should be bandaged – the tender skin under the burn could actually stick to the bandage and make the injury worse.

Cool the burnt area

Get the burn under cold water as soon as you can. Always try to get it under running water – if there is none, try pouring a bucket of water over, but be careful of stagnant pond water, which may be very dirty. As well as cooling the burn, the running water should help wash any dirt away.

Remove restrictions

Take off any watches or jewellery that may become tight if the area swells. Never remove any clothing that's stuck to a burn – you could do more damage.

Minor burns, where the skin has not blistered, can be gently dried with cotton wool and then covered with a loose bandage. A major burn, where there is blistering, or if the skin has broken and weeping, should not be bandaged but kept cool and damp with a wet cloth. Seek professional medical help as soon as you can.

Treating cuts

Small cuts can be treated easily in the wild, with antiseptic wipes and plasters — larger wounds should always be treated by medical professionals as soon as possible. Losing a little bit of blood isn't too much of a problem, but someone with a bad wound can lose a lot of blood very quickly. This can be very serious and they might even need a blood transfusion, to replace the lost blood.

1. Apply pressure to the wound to stop the bleeding. If it's a clean cut, try to raise it so the blood flows away from the wound.

2. Hold the edges together — or for larger cuts, press a clean pad firmly on to it.

3. Try to remove any thorns, shards of glass or dirt from small cuts. Do not try to remove objects from larger wounds as this may cause further serious bleeding.

4. Once the bleeding has slowed or stopped, keep the pad on and wind a bandage around the area.

5. Keep the bandage firm but not too tight — the idea is to keep the pressure on the wound without cutting off the blood supply.

6. Don't keep removing the bandage to check on the cut — the wound could get dirty and it might start bleeding again.

Frostbite

Frostbite affects parts of the body that are exposed, such as fingers, toes and nose. In extreme cases, the cells of the affected parts can die, and those bits can actually drop off!

Symptoms

- Pins and needles, throbbing and aching in the affected area.
- The skin becomes cold and white.
- If untreated, the skin will turn blue or blotchy.
- The affected parts will feel hard.
- As the skin warms, blisters may form and turn black. If untreated, this is when the most damage occurs and can result in amputation.

Treating frostbite

- Try to get out of the cold as soon as possible.
- Change out of any wet clothes into dry, warmer clothes.
- Wrap the patient in blankets.
- **DO NOT** rub the affected parts or hold them too close to a fire — this could cause further damage.
- Get a professional medic as soon as you can!

Hypothermia

Hypothermia happens when a person is exposed to cold for so long their body temperature lowers to a dangerous level. This means that the body will start to "shut down" in order to save energy.

Symptoms

- Shivering, cold skin, low energy
- Confusion, drowsiness, slurring
- Shallow breathing and a weak pulse
- If untreated, loss of consciousness

Treating hypothermia

- Find shelter or somewhere warm as soon as possible.
- Wrap blankets around the patient.

- Change out of wet clothing into dry clothes.
- If you can, use your own body heat to warm the patient — a hug works wonders!
- Try to give the patient warm (not burning hot) drinks and small amounts of chocolate.
- Seek medical attention as soon as you can!

Heat exhaustion

This happens when the body's temperature gets too hot. If untreated it can lead to heatstroke, which is when important parts of the body break down and stop working.

Symptoms

- Flushed, hot skin and heavy sweating
- Nausea and vomiting
- Extreme tiredness and a racing heartbeat
- Confusion
- Urinating less often and much darker than usual

Treating heat exhaustion

- Get the patient into the shade.
- Make sure they drink lots of water

(with rehydrating sachets if possible). Keep doing this until the symptoms have all gone.

- Cool the skin by wiping their face with a cold wet flannel.
- Loosen clothing.

Dehydration

This happens when the amount of water in your body drops to dangerous levels. Water makes up two-thirds of your body and a big drop in the amount you have can be very serious.

Symptoms

- The first sign is thirst
- Also look out for dizziness, and a light-headed feeling
- Headaches, tiredness
- Very dark urine, and needing to wee only rarely
- Very dry mouth and cracked lips

Treating dehydration

- Get the patient into the shade, and sitting down.
- Make them drink lots of water. Lots of little sips are much better than big gulps.
- If you have rehydration packets, use them!
- If the patient cannot keep the water down or has diarrhoea, seek medical attention as soon as possible.

Altitude sickness

This happens when you're so high that your body can't take in enough oxygen for your muscles, internal organs and brain to work properly. If left untreated it can be very serious.

Symptoms

- Mild altitude sickness starts with tiredness and a headache.
- Look out for nausea and dizziness following.
- Shortness of breath.
- Confusion and clumsiness are common.
- In severe cases, patients may cough up a frothy spit.

Treating altitude sickness

- Altitude sickness can be helped by not climbing too high too quickly – take the time to acclimatize.
- Drink plenty of liquid and stay hydrated.
- It is essential to get the patient back down the mountain as soon as possible.
- If symptoms still persist, get the patient to a hospital as soon as you can.

Make a sling

Slings are great for supporting arm injuries — they take the weight of the arm and help protect it from further knocks. Making one is easy — all you need is the triangular bandage in your first-aid kit.

1. Lay the bandage around the neck as shown, so the bigger part of the triangle hangs down the front.

2. Keep the hand of the injured arm higher than the elbow.

3. Raise the lower point of the bandage and tie it to the point on the shoulder.

4. Fold the last remaining flap at the elbow and attach it to the rest of the sling with a safety pin.

Make a crutch

Injured legs or feet can be helped with a simple home-made crutch. Simply find a strong stick with a fork at one end. Cut it so it's about the same length as the height from the ground to your chest. To use it, simply tuck the fork under your armpit, hold your injured leg off the ground and let the crutch take the weight on that side. Practise walking with a crutch at home before you set off on an adventure.

Make a stretcher

Stretchers are used to carry badly injured people safely — and with a little improvisation you can make your own in the wild.

- Turn two coats inside out and button or zip them up. Place them flat down, one in front of the other on the ground.
- Find two strong, straight poles — stiff tent poles are ideal — the bendy kind are no good.
- Pass the poles through the coat sleeves so the ends stick out.
- Always test a stretcher before you use it!

Importance of medical courses

Please do not think that just because you've read and understood a few basic first-aid techniques that you'll be prepared to cope with any emergency situation in the wild! Every emergency is different! The well-prepared adventurer will have attended at least one medical course and we recommend going on a "refresher" course before every long trip into the wild.

TRUE TALE: Aron Ralston

In 2003, mountain climber Aron Ralston was hiking alone through the remote Blue John Canyon in Utah, USA, when a huge boulder suddenly became dislodged and crashed against his right arm, pinning him to the canyon wall. Ralston hadn't told anyone where he was going, so he knew nobody would come to rescue him.

For five days, Ralston tried to work his arm free — but the boulder simply wouldn't budge. He had very little water, and as he grew ever more dehydrated and delirious he began to realize that if he was to escape, he'd have to do something drastic.

On the fifth day, the water ran out. Ralston carved his name, date of birth and that day's date into the canyon wall, and prepared to do the unthinkable. For the next hour, he sawed at his own arm with a half-blunt knife until finally he hacked it off just below the elbow. In incredible pain, and half-surprised he was still alive, he bandaged up the stump, climbed down the canyon wall and hiked across the desert. Eventually, a helicopter found and rescued him.

It's amazing Ralston survived at all, but what's more astounding is that it didn't put him off his love of the wild. Since the accident — and despite having only one arm — he's climbed several mountains, including Mount Kilimanjaro. And he still intends to climb Everest!

PART 9: REFERENCE

So by now you should have a pretty good understanding about the basics of how to go wild. So what are you waiting for? Get out there!

This last section contains some useful charts for converting distances and weights — as well as some amazing-but-true facts about the world outside your windows. Some of it may be useful, some of it can just be used to impress your friends!

Finally, there's a further reading list. If you've enjoyed hearing about some of history's greatest adventurers, be sure to check out the suggestions in your local library...

Conversion charts

Length
1 mile = 1.6 km
1 foot = 0.3 metres
1 inch = 2.54 cm

Area
1 square miles = 2.6 square km
1 square feet = 0.1 square metres
1 square inch = 6.5 square cm

Capacity
1 gallon = 4.5 litres
1 pint = 0.6 litres

Weight
1 pound = 0.5 kg
1 ounce = 28.3 g

Speed
1 mph = 1.6 km/h

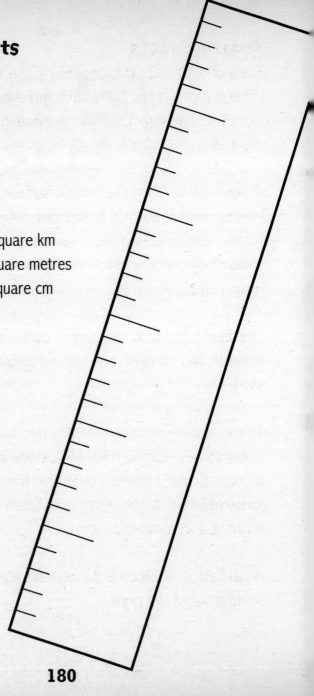

Amazing facts

Some of these facts may be useful in the wild – and some of them are just brilliant for impressing your mates with! But all of them show just what an amazing place the world we live in is...

Seventy per cent of the earth's surface is covered by oceans. That's why it's sometimes called the "Blue Planet". Only five per cent of these oceans have been explored by man – 95 per cent remains unseen by human eyes.

The Pacific Ocean is the largest ocean in the world. It has an area of around 70,000,000 square miles.

The longest river in the world is the Nile in Africa – it stretches nearly 6,700 km! However, due to arguments about where exactly the Nile starts, some believe that the Amazon in South America might be a few metres longer.

Angel Falls in Venezuela is the highest waterfall in the world at 3,212 feet high.

Lake Baikal in Russia is the world's oldest and deepest lake. It is thought to be 30 million years old and has an average depth of 744.4 metres – but at its deepest is 1,642 metres deep!

Lake Malawi in East Africa contains more fish species than any other lake.

The Amazon rainforest in South America is so big that it is thought to still contain many undiscovered tribes. It covers an area over five and a half million square km.

The largest living thing on earth isn't an animal … it's the Great Barrier Reef, off the coast of Australia. It is over 2,000 km long.

The Pantanal wetlands in South America are the largest wetlands in the world – home to giant waterlilies, underwater forests and over 300 species of fish, including red bellied piranha.

Every winter in the Antarctic the ice advances four km per day and the continent doubles in size in just a few weeks.

The Sahara desert in Africa is the same size as the USA. The vast amounts of sand and dust found there can be blown 5,000 metres up into the sky.

The biggest desert in the world is not the Sahara — as a desert is any area which receives a tiny amount of rainfall a year, then technically the biggest desert in the world is actually Antarctica!

The highest mountains in the world are the Himalayas. The range is over 3,000 km long with hundreds of peaks measuring over 7,000 metres tall and 13 mountains over 8,000 metres high.

The highest mountain in the world is Mount Everest, which stands 8,848 metres above sea level.

The Krubera Cave in Georgia is the deepest cave in the world — descending 2,191 metres — meaning the Empire State Building could fit in it nearly five times!

There are more insects in the world than all the other animals added together.

The combined weight of all the ants in the world is about the same as the combined weight of all the humans.

The poison arrow frog — found in Central and South America — is the most poisonous animal in the world.

Polar bears can run at nearly 30 mph and jump over six feet in the air.

The earth is always travelling around the sun — at a speed of 106,216 km/h. It is also rotating at a pretty speedy 1600 km/h.

One orbit of the sun means the earth travels nearly 939,000,000 miles.

One day doesn't actually last 24 hours: the exact time it takes the earth to rotate fully is 23 hours, 56 minutes and 4 seconds. And a year isn't actually 365 days, but 365.25 days. That's why we have leap years every four years.

Light from the sun takes about eight minutes to reach us. So when you look at the sun, technically, you're seeing it as it was eight minutes ago!

The highest temperature ever recorded on earth was 57.78°C in Libya in 1922.

The lowest temperature ever recorded on earth was -89.22°C in Antarctica in 1983.

Wild wisdom

You know those old sayings – red sky at night, shepherd's delight, and so on? Ever wondered where they come from? The truth is that they didn't happen by accident – all of the best ones came about from old adventurers', farmers' and explorers' experience.

Here's a selection of the most reliable…

* When the dew is on the grass, rain will never come to pass.
* When grass is dry at morning light, look for rain before the night.
* Rain before seven, clear at eleven.
* Swallows flying low means rain, flying high means clear again.
* A deep, clear sky of fleckless blue, brings storms within a day or two.
* When the wind is in the east, it's good for neither man nor beast.
* When the wind is in the north, the old folk should not venture forth.
* When the wind is in the south, it blows the bait in the fish's mouth.
* When the wind is in the west, it is of all the winds the best.

Further reading list

If you enjoyed hearing about the real life adventurers in this book, you might want to look out for the following books for more amazing stories about the same characters…

Robinson Crusoe by Daniel Defoe

Cassell's Tales of Endurance by Fergus Fleming

The Travels of Marco Polo by Marco Polo

Scouting for Boys by Robert Baden Powell

Harriet Chalmers-Adams: Adventurer and Explorer by Durlynn Anema

The Incredible Outback Adventure of Burke and Wills by Frank Clune

The Story of Scott and the Race to the South Pole by Jim Pipe

Kon-Tiki: Across the Pacific in a Raft by Thor Heyerdahl

Davy Crockett: Frontier Legend by George Edward Stanley

Extreme Exploration by John Malam

127 Hours: Between a Rock and a Hard Place by Aron Ralston

Daniel Boone: Woodsman of Kentucky by John Paul Zronik

The Last of the Mohicans by James Fenimore Cooper

The Man Eaters of Tsavo by John Henry Patterson

Great Explorers by David Angus

OUT NOW

HOW TO MAKE
MONEY

Smart ways to make MILLIONS

SELL
LEMONADE

STAGE A
CONCERT

FIND
TREASURE

START A
CRAZE

BOSS

CHRISTOPHER EDGE